D1806292

# Equalities
## and Inequalities
### in Education

# Equalities and Inequalities in Education

*Proceedings of the Eleventh Annual
Symposium of the Eugenics Society
London 1974*

*Edited by*

## PETER R. COX
*Government Actuary's Department,
London*

## H. B. MILES
*The University, Hull*

## JOHN PEEL
*Teesside Polytechnic,
Middlesbrough, Teesside*

1975

## Academic Press
## London · New York · San Francisco
*A Subsidiary of Harcourt Brace Jovanovich, Publishers*

ACADEMIC PRESS INC. (LONDON) LTD.
24/28 Oval Road,
London NW1

*United States Edition published by*
ACADEMIC PRESS INC.
111 Fifth Avenue
New York, New York 10003

Library of Congress Catalog Card Number: 75-19627
ISBN: 0-12-194240-6

PRINTED IN GREAT BRITAIN BY
UNWIN BROTHERS LIMITED
THE GRESHAM PRESS, OLD WOKING, SURREY
A MEMBER OF THE STAPLES PRINTING GROUP

# Contributors

W. H. G. ARMYTAGE, *Department of Education, University of Sheffield, Sheffield S10 2TN, England*

J. A. BEARDMORE, *Department of Genetics, University College of Swansea, Swansea SA2 8PP, South Wales*

B. BENJAMIN, *Department of Social Science and Humanities, The City University, St. John Street, London EC1V 4PB, England*

JEAN FLOUD, *Newnham College, Cambridge CB3 9HQ, England*

A. G. HEARNDEN, *Department of Comparative Education, University of London Institute of Education, Malet Street, London WC1E 7HS, England*

S. B. MARSH, *Department of Law, Manchester Polytechnic, Aytoun Street, Manchester M1 3GH, England*

D. L. NUTTALL, *Schools Council, 160 Great Portland Street, London W1N 6LL, England*

J. T. PARK, *Department of Adult Education and Extramural Studies, Liberal Studies Division, The University, Leeds LS2 9JT, England*

P. B. RATTENBURY, *Department of Education and Science, Elizabeth House, York Road, London, SE1 7PH, England*

B. SIMON, *School of Education, University of Leicester, Leicester LE1 7RF, England*

W. D. WALL, *Department of Child Development and Educational Psychology, University of London Institute of Education, 24 & 27 Woburn Square, London WC1H 0AA, England*

E. WILKES, *Department of Community Medicine, University of Sheffield Medical School, Beech Hill Road, Sheffield S10 2RX, England*

# Preface

This volume records the proceedings of the eleventh Symposium of the Eugenics Society. Its theme is equality and inequality in education.

Widespread social concern about education and its social effects has been prominent in public debate in this country for more than a decade. During that time several previous symposia of the Eugenics Society, covering various socio-biological aspects of contemporary problems, have included a number of papers having direct or indirect educational relevance (notably the second symposium on Genetic and Environmental Factors in Human Ability). However, the issues under debate have recently appeared to be even further from resolution than they were ten years ago and beliefs held earlier on the potential influence of education as a tool of social engineering have come to be regarded by some (including dedicated reformists) as naive and contradicted by research evidence. During the same period numbers of students in higher education have doubled and the traditional role and nature of institutions of higher education have been called in question. There have also been heartsearchings about the adequacy of prevailing methods of preparation for the professions and public service with a general groundswell of movement towards revision and reform. In short, education at all levels is increasingly a matter of general concern and the Council of the Society felt that the time was opportune to make education the focus of a Symposium.

As the members of Council responsible for the structure of the Symposium we take formal responsibility for the editing of the volume but the day-to-day work has fallen on the shoulders of Miss Eileen Walters, General Secretary of the Eugenics Society, and this we acknowledge gladly and with thanks.

*On behalf of the Eugenics Society*
P. R. Cox
H. B. Miles
July 1975
J. Peel

vii

# Contents

# Biological Inequality and Education

## J. A. BEARDMORE

*Department of Genetics,*
*University College of Swansea, University of Wales, Wales*

"It is a human characteristic to give reasons which will not bear examination for the most sensible actions. Many Polynesians are only kept from theft by the belief that if they violate the taboo attaching to the coconuts of their neighbours they will be struck dead. Some fundamentalists (at least in England) hold that a belief in Noah's ark is a necessary preliminary to a good life. In mediaeval Europe it was only possible to centralize government as a result of a belief in the divine institution of monarchy, which was later formulated as the divine right of kings.

And in the present age the admirable institution of universal suffrage is similarly supported by the curious dogma of the equality of man. Historically this dogma arose as a protest against institutions such as hereditary rank, which still commands the respect of the readers of the social columns of British newspapers, and of the daughters of American millionaires. But if the framers of the American Constitution subscribed to the theory of the equality of man, the true founders of the nation, the Pilgrim Fathers, held the opposite doctrine in its most extreme form. They were Calvinists and believed that human beings, from the moment of birth, were segregated into two distinct categories, the one predestined to eternal bliss, the other to everlasting damnation."

The words above are not the creation of a student of politics or sociology. They were written over forty years ago in an essay entitled "The Inequality of Man", by one of the great men of twentieth century British biology, J. B. S. Haldane, who combined great powers of analysis and insight with a very highly developed social conscience and very left-wing political sympathies (Haldane, 1932).

A few of his other observations on broad cultural and educational matters will, I think, bear repeating. Some are highly provocative, e.g.

"Between 3000 B.C. and A.D. 1400, there were probably only four really important inventions, namely, the general use of iron, paved roads, voting, and religious intolerance."

1

Others are highly relevant to this Symposium.

"The child represents the hope of humanity. We are not giving our children a fair deal. Many of those who could benefit most from higher education do not get it. Others are given more education than they either want or can assimilate. Hardly any are introduced to the scientific outlook until their minds have been so filled with pre-scientific ideas as to make scientific thought very difficult. I think that justice for children is even more important than justice for adults. As a biologist, I realize that all men are different, and I do not offer my thoughts as a pattern for others.

"The progress of biology in the next century will lead to a recognition of the innate inequality of man. This is today most obviously visible in the United States, where educational opportunities are more widespread than elsewhere. Universal education leads, not to equality but to inequality based on real differences of talent. Where there is equality of opportunity, there is no excuse for failure."

Haldane's thoughts, even at this distance of time, provide a good starting point for a discussion which considers the significance of modern biological knowledge for the theme of equalities and inequalities in education. Equality is itself a word which conveys different things to different people. In this discussion I have taken biological equality to mean what the Oxford dictionary refers to as "the same in number, size, degree, etc." and not what it presumably meant to the framers of the imperishable phrase "All men are created equal" and indeed to many other people, i.e. the same in merit. We may note that not all biologists would agree with this distinction (Dobzhansky, 1968) and as it is well known that considerable problems arise from trying to reconcile political equality with cultural or economic equality it is not surprising that similar difficulties should exist in connection with biological inequality. It is also interesting that, as Provine (1973) has pointed out, ideas about hereditary differences in mental attributes can change considerably over a period when little additional information becomes available.

It is probably true that, about the time that Haldane's essay was written, some of the seeds leading to the blossoming of the 1944 Education Act in Britain were being set. Key phrases in the development of thinking leading to this legislation are "parity of esteem" and (one mentioned by Haldane) "equality of opportunity".

The concepts that lie behind these phrases continue to be important and have been of crucial importance in shaping the pattern of evolution to comprehensive education in secondary education which has so far taken place in Britain. They also apply in some measure to higher education in which polytechnics and the Open University have developed alongside the established universities and, in the USA and other European countries, have led to the beginnings of comprehensive universities (Embling, 1974).

However, the precise meaning of equality in an educational context continues to be variable and elusive as the following sample of comments may show.

*Lord Boyle*

1. "The essential point is that all children should have equal opportunity of acquiring intelligence and developing their talents and abilities to the full." (Newsom, 1963.)

*R. Prentice* (as Minister for Education)

2. "Equality entails an element of positive discrimination in favour of disadvantaged children. It does not mean that people are equal and must be subjected to a cultural uniformity." (Devlin, 1974.)

3. "The supply of superior intelligence is limited and the demand for it in society is even greater. The largest unused supply is found among women." (Embling, 1974) (The conclusion about inequality of treatment is clear.)

*US undergraduates* (some)

4. "All grades should be abolished." (Embling, 1974.)

*Italian undergraduates* (some)

5. "In some university institutions examinations may be conducted orally by an examiner with a group of students who have themselves chosen the members of the group. The performance of the group as a whole is determined by the answers given by individuals (sometimes only one individual) so that the performance of one good student can result in good assessments being given to ten others, some of whom may be very poor." (Related to me by Dr G. C. Fava.)

I would like now to discuss briefly what is known of the range of biological inequalities. By this, I mean those differences between individuals which arise from the fact that they possess different genetic endowments.

There are, first of all, individuals whose make-up of genes or chromosomes is such as inevitably to handicap them in a major way. One example of this type is comprised by those unfortunate enough to possess an extra chromosome 21, known as Down's syndrome, in which a widespread collection of deviations from normal physical and mental performance are manifest. Another example is that of individuals suffering from phenylketonuria as a result of the possession of a double dose of a particular recessive mutant gene. Fortunately, this disease is amenable to treatment but, if untreated, leads to severe loss of mental function. It is, however, but one of a large class of genetic diseases which, whilst individually rare, constitute together a significant fraction of the population.

Another cause of biological inequality arises from the presence in our society of those conditions such as *spina bifida* in which a significant handicap to normal education will often exist and in which genetic factors are certainly causally implicated but where there is a complex interaction of genetic and environmental factors effective in producing the condition.

There is likely to be little argument that individuals handicapped in ways such as those described above will usually need special educational opportunities of kinds which are different from those experienced by the majority of the population, though it is to be hoped that, as time progresses, effective treatment of more of the conditions with a simple genetic basis will become possible and that affected children will not need special educational measures.

The third type of biological inequality to which I wish to refer is that of the division of our species into two sexes. Indeed this division is the most obvious kind of biological inequality. The mechanism which determines sex is basically simple and involves a difference in one of the forty-six chromosomes characteristically present in each of the body cells of man. As the chromosomes carry the genetic information passed from generation to generation, it is indisputable that there is a real, innate difference between males and females (though the evidence of our eyes is sufficient to convince most of us of that anyway). In some of the genes carried on sex chromosomes there are differences between the sexes relevant to education. For example colour blindness is very rare in women because the gene controlling it is recessive and two doses of the gene are needed. In men, who have only one X-chromosome, the gene is expressed in all individuals carrying it. There are also differences of survival (Potts, 1970) of hormonal balance, likely to influence learning, cognition and memory and there are probably important differences in neural function in the sexes which are traceable back to very early stages in development (Marshall, 1970).

It is commonly held that measures of average overall ability and achievement in males and females show little difference in mean although in performing specific tasks quite marked differences may be found. For example, males generally score more highly on spatial and numerical tests whilst females generally score more highly on verbal tests (Dale, 1970). Good evidence for genetic determination of spatial ability is available (Bock and Kolakowski, 1973) and an interesting connection between spatial ability and vertical accuracy in throwing ability has been linked to selective pressures in the hunting phase of man's evolution (Kolakowski and Malina, 1974).

More significant, perhaps, than such differences in mean is the fact that the distribution around the mean tends to be less variable for females and more variable for males. Thus, there are said to be more highly intelligent and highly unintelligent males than females. It can be argued that this difference in variance applies to many aspects of behaviour and is the main reason for the great preponderance of males in the outstanding figures in many fields of human activity. I do not, of course, pretend that cultural differences can be excluded as causes of some of this important difference in variability (which, incidently, seems to be ignored or treated as a nuisance by many students of educational psychology, e.g. Vernon, 1969). However, accepting that substantial and discriminatory differences in the treatment of males and females exist does not provide an explanation of this difference in variance it could account for differences of mean. Such differences in variance may be very great, for example it has been shown that in large samples the variance in tests of spatial ability was almost twice as large for boys as for girls (Bock and Kolakowski, 1973).

Other relevant examples of this difference can be cited. Broadhead (1972), in a survey of all children in a large area of the USA found children who had minimal brain injury or were educationally subnormal were twice as common among boys as among girls (Table I). This suggests very strongly that there is greater spread of underlying variability determining risk to such conditions among boys.

### TABLE I

*Sex differences in the incidence of children in special education (Broadhead, 1972)*

|  | Girls | Boys |
|---|---|---|
| ESN | 109 | 152 |
| MBI | 47 | 159 |
|  | 156 | 311 |

The statistical supplement to the eleventh UCCA report provides another piece of useful data. Table II shows the distribution of A-level scores for all UK university entrants for the year 1972–73.

## TABLE II

### The distribution (%) of A-level scores (A = 5, B = 4 etc.) by sex in university entrants 1972-73 (UCCA, 1974)

| A-level score | <9 | 9–12 | >12 | N |
|---|---|---|---|---|
| Girls | 24 | 49 | 27 | 1644 |
| Boys | 28 | 43 | 29 | 2779 |

The mean score is, if anything, slightly higher for the girls but the distribution of female scores is less variable than that for the male students.

Although there is clearly scope for more critical data to be gathered it seems likely to me that this difference in variability of the sexes is a fundamental one of some significance for education.

The last type of biological variation is that which we can call normal populational variation. The recognition of such variation springs from the fact that in recent years we have come to realize that man is genetically very diverse. There are, of course, obvious differences between certain groups of people but, even within what might, in a general way, be regarded as a homogeneous population, there is a very considerable amount of genetic variation. Broadly, it seems that roughly one-third of the gene loci in a population such as that of Britain, are represented by two or more forms of gene concerned (Harris and Hopkinson, 1972). The result of this widespread genetic variability is that we can be quite sure that all individuals (the two members of an identical twin pair excepted) are genetically unique (Beardmore, 1974).

This view of the structure of a population as consisting of an array of essentially different individuals is of immense importance. It shows us that, in a biological sense, far from all men being equal all men are unequal (and some more so than others). However, it can reasonably be asked whether the blood groups, serum and tissue enzymes, eye colours and other characteristics variable for genetic reasons influence those aspects of human behaviour important in the educational process.

Unfortunately, little is known directly of the nature or number of the genes controlling the distribution of properties such as intelligence, drive and creative or mechanical skills, which together may be termed educability (Thoday, 1972) the potential of which an educational system seeks to realize as completely as possible. It is therefore extremely difficult to judge to what extent the degree of genetic diversity for, say, blood groups within one population parallels genetic diversity for educability. On general grounds, however, this seems likely.

It seems highly probable, furthermore, that much of the observed variation seen in our imperfect attempts to measure such attributes by means of IQ tests and the like is genetic in origin (Jinks and Fulker, 1970; Scarr Salapatek, 1974).

The evidence which supports this statement is based upon many studies in which correlations between relatives are examined. In studies of children adopted at any early age, it has been clearly demonstrated that the IQ of the children was much more highly correlated with the educational level reached by the biological parents than with that of the adoptive parents. Furthermore, the difference became greater with the age of the child so that at age fourteen years the correlation with biological parents was about $0.35$ while that with adoptive parents was only about $0.05$ (Honzik, 1957; Skodak and Skeels, 1949).

More compelling evidence, however, comes from the large study by Erlenmeyer-Kimling and Jarvik (1963) in which the results of many such investigations, using a variety of different techniques in a number of different countries and extending over several decades, are combined.

Some interesting work indicating that normal populational variation in protein and blood group genes may be significant in this context is provided by the work of Gibson et al. (1973) who examined the IQ of individuals from an Oxfordshire population also typed for their ABO blood group. The results showed that the mean IQs of individuals with the $A_2$ or O phenotype are significantly higher than the mean IQ of $A_1$ individuals. The sample size is relatively small and more work is needed to be sure of the reality of the observed difference but the implications of the data are important for our theme, particularly as there are appreciable geographic differences in the distribution of ABO types even within the UK.

As so much data on IQ is available it is not surprising that so much discussion about educability should involve it. Many other factors are, however, likely to be involved in moulding educability in specific individuals. In particular tests of components of creative ability appear to show that while there may be highly significant correlations between some of these components and IQ (e.g. figure production) in the main the correlations are low or non-significant (Johnson and Fogel, 1974). However, other work suggests that creative ability is linked with personality type and hence heritable variation between individuals is likely to be involved (Götz and Götz, 1973).

## TABLE III

*Correlation coefficients for IQ and genetic correlations for various comparisons. The correlation for IQ is the median value of all the studies in each comparison (Erlenmeyer-Kimling and Jarvik, 1963)*

| Relationship | | Correlation coefficient IQ | Genetic correlation | No. of studies |
|---|---|---|---|---|
| Unrelated | Reared apart | −0·01 | 0·0 | 4 |
| | Reared together | 0·23 | 0·0 | 5 |
| Foster-parent child | | 0·22 | 0·0 | 3 |
| Parent child | | 0·50 | 0·5 | 12 |
| Siblings | Reared apart | 0·40 | 0·5 | 2 |
| | Reared together | 0·49 | 0·5 | 35 |
| Dizygote twins | Unlike sex | 0·53 | 0·5 | 9 |
| | Like sex | 0·53 | 0·5 | 11 |
| Monozygote twins | Reared apart | 0·75 | 1·0 | 4 |
| | Reared together | 0·87 | 1·0 | 14 |

If it is accepted that there is likely to be considerable genetic variation influencing educability in any population even if individual genes cannot, for the present, be identified and located it is of considerable interest to ask what biological factors are important in determining the distribution of such genes. There are probably a great many such factors but of these the most important and interesting for the present discussion are natural selection, differential migration, social mobility, assortative mating and inbreeding.

The effects of natural selection are quite simply to increase generation by generation the frequencies of those genetic constitutions which survive and reproduce more efficiently (i.e. those having greater Darwinian fitness). Such survival and reproductive efficiency in any given population is dependent upon the nature of the environment inhabited by that population and much, if not all, of the genetic differences between, say, Australian aboriginal, Japanese and Irish populations is likely to be the result of natural selection favouring different gene complexes having adaptive significance in different environments. Such genetic differences will often be statistical rather than such as to distinguish all individuals of one group from all individuals of another group but would be expected to involve both physical and mental attributes. Any detectable relationship between Darwinian fitness and educability would, of course, be of considerable interest. Recent evidence on the fertility of IQ groups from the USA (Bajema, 1971) suggests that average fertility is greatest in two groups, those with IQs of greater than 120 and those in the 80–94 range (Table IV). Extrapolation from these data would however be difficult without further evidence.

## TABLE IV
### Relative fitness in relation to IQ (from Bajema, 1971)

| IQ Range | Relative fitness |
|---|---|
| 120 | 1·000 |
| 105–119 | 0·867 |
| 95–104 | 0·784 |
| 80–94 | 0·960 |
| 69–79 | 0·584 |

The effects of differential migration are easily visualized; if either high or low educability genotypes leave a population in disproportionate numbers the mean educability level of the population should correspondingly fall or rise. It is often assumed that emigrants comprise a disproportionately large fraction of able individuals (Eysenck, 1971) but critical data are hard to come by (McGonigle and McPhilemy, 1974).

By social mobility, we understand the movement of individuals from one social subsection of the population to another and, usually, social classes are the subsections considered (Halsey, 1972). The significance of social mobility for the present discussion is that social mobility is associated with IQ and social class is also associated with IQ. Thus Gibson (1970) has shown, in a sample of Cambridge scientists, that a direct correspondence exists between the amount of social mobility and the differences in IQ between the scientists and their fathers. As there is a large heritable component in IQ, this indicates that social classes are almost certainly genetically differentiated from each other to some extent.

The implications of this argument are, of course, profound and have been discussed at length by Herrnstein (1973) and Eysenck (1973) among others. First, as social mobility is probably increasing, the degree of sorting out of genes is probably becoming greater, i.e. classes based more and more on intelligence levels will tend to become more genetically differentiated from one another. Simulated laboratory experiments have shown that, for a character showing a normal distribution, it is possible with about 25% social mobility and a two-class system to produce, within ten generations, a population in which the genetic differences between classes are larger than those within classes (Thoday and Gibson, 1970). Implications of this argument for topics such as ESN education, compensatory education (Chazan, 1973) and neighbourhood schools are fairly obvious.

The tendency of like to marry like is known as assortative mating. Its strength can be measured on a scale which uses the correlation between mates for the character in question. It is well known that in Man assortative mating for educational level, for intelligence, for age, and some personality attributes takes place (McClearn and De Fries, 1973) though not all to the same extent and quite possibly not to the same extent for any one character in various parts of the population. For intelligence, the correlation between spouses is of the order of $0 \cdot 5$. As there are also strong social class correlations in choice of mate (64% in a recent survey in Oxfordshire), such assortative mating clearly leads to a stabilizing effect on the distribution of the genes in a social class, although when the assortative mating for intelligence is coupled with social mobility this will clearly not apply.

Another example of non-random choice of mates is that of inbreeding, that is mating of relatives. In practical terms matings between relatives produce children who are, on average, rather more homozygous than the population mean to an extent depending on the intensity of inbreeding. Thus, first cousin matings produce a more marked increase in homozygosity in the offspring than second cousin matings.

Data from extensive studies in Japan have shown that the children of such matings are significantly lower in performance of a number of WISC components, when effects of age and SES are removed, the verbal score being $2 \cdot 76\%$ lower and performance score $2 \cdot 06\%$ lower (Schull and Neel, 1965). Thus, in any area where inbreeding occurs, it is to be expected that the average genetic potential of the children produced will be somewhat lower.

In conclusion I hope to have shown that there are a number of aspects of biological variation which ought to be taken into account when formulating and implementing educational policies. The genetic uniqueness of the individual expressed as subtle variations in ambitions, drive, social relations with others and abilities of various kinds means that no single treatment will do exactly the same for all people. "Education is to Man what manure is to the Pea", remarked an eminent British geneticist shortly after the birth of his science (Punnett, 1907) but different genetic types of pea react differently to the presence of a shovelful of the same manure and different genetic types of man will react differently to the same packet of education. Furthermore, while we have little difficulty in defining how we wish our peas to look and to taste there is obviously much less agreement as to what the end result of the educational process ought to be, at least in measurable terms.

Clearly the interactions of genetic and cultural factors which bring about behavioural variations between individuals are still only understood in a fragmentary way. However, it seems evident to me that only when the reality and the extent of genetic differences, first and most importantly between individuals, then between the sexes, and then between social or other groups of individuals, is recognized, will a good educational system permit what I judge to be a widely accepted goal to be reached; that is to make possible the development to the fullest extent of each individual's ability and aspirations.

## Acknowledgement

My thanks are due to Mr M. Chazan, Mr R. R. Dale and Professor R. H. Pritchard for helpful discussions.

## References

Bajema, C. J. (1971). Estimation of the direction and intensity of Natural Selection in relation to human intelligence by means of the intrusive rate of natural increase. In *Natural Selection in Human Populations*. Edited by C. J. Bajema. Pp. 276–291. New York: Wiley.

Beardmore, J. A. (1974). Genetic consequences and problems of the new biology. In *Population and the New Biology*. Edited by B. Benjamin, P. R. Cox and J. Peel. pp. 105–118. London: Academic Press.

Bock, R. D. and Kolakowski, D. (1973). Further evidence of sex-linked major gene influence on human spatial visualizing ability. *American Journal of Human Genetics*, **25**, 1–14.

Broadhead, G. D. (1972). Social class factors in special education. *Journal of Biosocial Science*, **4**, 315–324.

Chazan, M. (Editor) (1973). *Compensatory Education*. London: Butterworth.

Dale, R. R. (1970). A comparison of the academic performance of male and female students in schools and universities. *Journal of Biosocial Science*, Suppl. 2, 95–100.

Devlin, T. (1974). What equality in education means to Mr. Prentice. *The Times*. 5 August.

Dobzhansky, Th. (1968). On genetics and politics. *Social Education*, **32**, 142–146.

Embling, J. (1974). *A Fresh Look at Higher Education*. Amsterdam, London, New York: Elsevier Scientific Publishing Co.

Erlenmeyer-Kimling, L. and Jarvik, L. F. (1963). Genetics and intelligence: a review. *Science*, **142**, 1,477–9.

Eysenck, H. J. (1971). *Race, Intelligence and Education*. London: Temple Smith.

Eysenck, H. J. (1973). *The Inequality of Man*. London: Temple Smith.

Gibson, J. B. (1970). Biological aspects of a high socio-economic group I IQ, education and social mobility. *Journal of Biosocial Science*, **2**, 1–16.

Gibson, J. B., Harrison, G. A., Clarke, C. A. and Hiorns, R. W. (1973). Existence of relationship between IQ and ABO blood groups. *Nature*, **246**, 498–499.

Götz, K. O. and Götz, K. (1973). Introversion-extroversion and neuroticism in gifted and ungifted art students. *Perceptual and Motor Sciences*, **36**, 675–687.

Haldane, J. B. S. (1932). *The Inequality of Man and Other Essays*. Harmondsworth, Middlesex: Penguin Books.

Halsey, A. H. (1972). *Social Mobility in the Structure of Human Populations*. Edited by G. A. Harrison and A. J. Boyle. Oxford: Clarendon Press.

Harris, H. and Hopkinson, D. A. (1972). Average heterozygosity per locus in man. An estimate based on the incidence of protein polymorphism. *Annals of Human Genetics*, **36**, 9–20.

Herrnstein, R. J. (1973). *IQ in the Meritocracy*. London: Allen Lane.

Honzik, M. P. (1957). Developmental studies of parent-child resemblance in intelligence. *Child Development*, **28**, 216–228.

Jinks, J. L. and Fulker, D. V. (1970). Comparisons of the biometrical and genetical, MAVA and classical approaches to the analysis of human behaviour. *Psychol. Bull.*, **73**, 311–349.

Johnson, D. and Fogel, M. (1974). Creative aptitudes in a high intelligence population. *Journal of General Psychology*, **91**, 93–104.

Kolakowski, D. and Malina, R. M. (1974). Spatial ability throwing accuracy and man's hunting heritage. *Nature*, **251**, 410–412.

McClearn, G. E. and De Fries, J. C. (1973). *Introduction to Behavioural Genetics*. San Francisco: Freeman.

McGonigle, B. and McPhilemy, S. (1974). Dispelling the mist around an Irish myth. *The Times Higher Ed. Suppl.*, **158**, 14.

Marshall, W. A. (1970). Sex differences at puberty. *Journal of Biosocial Science*, Suppl. 2, 31–42.

Newsom, Sir J. (1963). *Half our Future*. Report of the Central Advisory Council for Education. London: HMSO.

Potts, D. M. (1970). Which is the 'weaker sex'? *Journal of Biosocial Science*, Suppl. 2. 147–157.

Provine, W. B. (1973). Geneticists and the biology of race crossing. *Science*, **182**, 790–796.

Punnett, R. C. (1907). *Mendelism*. Cambridge: Bowes and Bowes.

Scarr Salapatek, S. (1974). Some myths about heritability and IQ. *Nature*, **251**, 463–464.

Schull, W. J. and Neel, J. V. (1965). *The Effects of Inbreeding on Japanese children*. New York: Harper and Row.

Skodak, M. and Skeels, H. M. (1949). A final follow-up study of one hundred adopted children. *Journal of Genetic Psychology*, **75,** 85–125.

Thoday, J. M. (1972). Genetics and educability. *Journal of Biological Education*, **6,** 323–329.

Thoday, J. M. and Gibson, J. B. (1970). Environmental and genetical contributions to class difference: a model experiment. *Science*, **167,** 990–992.

UCCA (1974). *Statistical supplement to the eleventh report* 1972–73. Cheltenham: UCCA.

Vernon, P. E. (1969). *Intelligence and Cultural Environment*. London: Methuen.

# The Psychology of Primary Education

## W. D. WALL

*Department of Child Development and Educational Psychology,
Institute of Education, University of London, London, England*

## Introduction

A paper as short as this purporting to deal with what has become a vast and controversial field must inevitably be somewhat sketchy, selective and incomplete. Moreover what might be called the psychology of the primary school must in fact stray into social psychology as well as developmental psychology and, since education is an applied field must also bear in mind the philosophical and social frameworks within which the school works and which to some extent condition even our research work in the broad field of human growth.

It should also be made clear at the outset that what is being talked about is not the first five or six years of compulsory schooling, but the first decade of life in which the school, the pre-school institutions, and the family, play interlocking parts. Roughly, in Piagetian (Piaget, 1947) terms, this is a period in which the child accedes, more or less well, to concrete operational thinking through the interaction of his maturing organism with a series of environments and towards the end of which some children at least have embarked upon formal operational thinking. It is a period during which largely because of radical imperfections in his thinking his cognitive and emotional development are considerably at risk; and one in which he has many "growth tasks" to achieve some of which are structured by the school in sequential ways, some of which are broadly determined by his culture and some of which are very much established in terms of parental expectations idiosyncratic to particular families.

Finally it should be said that, in what follows, the attempt will be made to distinguish between what are facts fairly well established by research and the inferences (and propagandist claims) based upon

15

them. These will be dealt with under three broad headings or categories: the differences which exist at entry to compulsory school between individuals and between groups; such inferences as we are entitled to make as to the origins of these differences; and how far the school does or can modify such differences.

## Individual Differences at School Entry

The first set of facts with which we have to deal is that which suggests that at the age of five or thereabouts children are as various as they are at any time except possibly in early adolescence. These differences strike teachers in terms of speech and the ability to communicate through speech—differences of two years or more in vocabulary development, in the role of language in communication with other children or adults, in qualitative use of language (Bernstein's restricted and elaborated codes) and so on. There are also quite striking differences in competence—in the skill with which a child interacts with other children and with adults, in how he or she handles materials of various kinds, in ability to think, learn and remember. Behind and underlying these, there will also be marked differences of a value-attitudinal kind, pro- and anti-school, immediate versus delayed gratifications, readiness to accept an adult other than mother and so on. In some ways the most marked and important for early schooling are those differences concerned with attitudinal readiness—readiness to accept instructions given to a group, ability to set a goal and work towards it without undue distractibility, sufficient social maturity for the child to be able to play with, rather than merely alongside, other children.

Many of these differences, if not all, are broadly related to socio-economic background—the variable with the most obstinate correlation with all indices of success in learning from reading and arithmetic to adjustment and mental health (Reuchlin and Lézine, 1972). Within this broad socio-economic variable, the crucial aspect seems not so much to be income or even father's job, but the level of parental education (particularly that of mother) and the rearing styles adopted. One should note too that although such things as mean levels of reading or verbal intelligence decline fairly regularly as one goes down in socio-economic level, the very big divide for all kinds of aspects of development is that between social groups I, II and III Non-manual and social groups III Manual, IV and V (Davie et al., 1972).

Further, and this is a fact which must give pause to those who pin a wide eyed faith on education in schools, a great many researches, the most recent being those connected with and following on the Plowden

Committee (Douglas, 1964; Douglas *et al.*, 1968), underline that the influence of the home is some two to three times as strong as that of the school on all aspects of cognitive development. Nevertheless we also find that, within very broad limits, whatever the kind and quality of the primary school, whatever form of organization it adopts—streamed or unstreamed, traditional or "progressive"—the differences existing initially tend to get wider as school progresses and continue to show themselves at the secondary stage (Central Advisory Council for Education, 1967; Peaker, 1971). There are two relatively important modifications to this last statement both of them, however, bearing upon the parental factors. Crude measures of "parental interest" seem to correlate with some upward modification particularly in social group III Non-manual and in the middle and lower groups, children of upwardly mobile parents tend to be improvers (Douglas, 1964).

So far we have been talking of what might be called the range of difference in normal groups. There are however two other broad groupings of children whose development is at risk and who, if no successful positive action is taken are likely to be severely disadvantaged and to fail to draw whatever benefit formal education can give them. The first of these are children who are at risk for social reasons: the child in the one parent family, or in a large family, or who lives in overcrowded conditions or where there are severe psychiatric conditions affecting one or both parents. The second group are those who have some physical, sensory or neurological handicap of a marked kind or a constellation of apparently minor handicaps—marginal brain damage, clumsiness, developmental lags and so on. Not infrequently such handicaps are coupled with various forms of social disadvantage and form part of a marginal syndrome in which helpless or hopeless parents fail to .take advantage of the health and social services or the handicaps themselves escape attention because they are apparently slight, until marked failure in school draws attention to them. Physical or sensory handicap, even when it is slight, interferes with the child's easy and systematic contact with the environment and thus impedes the learning on which the early structuring of "intelligence" depends. A combination of adverse factors, each one relatively minor in itself, is nearly always found in the background of children who experience difficulty in school (Morris, 1966).

## So-called Cultural Disadvantage

By way of an extensive parenthesis, something should be said of the culturally disadvantaged. This is something of a misty and emotive concept and in one interpretation would include all those whose background is not in accord with the expectations of the school (which are characterized by some as "middle class"). The inference frequently made is that somehow the school should change its expectations and move more towards "working class" value systems and motivations and in effect provide a different education for working class or other culturally deprived or culturally different groups. Such a stance begs important questions about such things as the importance, absolutely and relatively, to modern communities of, for example, verbal symbolic thinking, delayed gratifications, rational judgment and the like which, although associated with the middle classes do not seem necessarily to be middle class. To go further in such a discussion would take us into the sociology and philosophy of knowledge, which is not our present purpose.

However, whatever stance we take, the concept of disadvantage needs rather careful spelling out. There seem to be three groups which can be distinguished for purposes of discussion, although in the case of any individual child, there may be and usually are extensive overlaps. The first might best be called *cultural difference*. The clearest and most obvious case is that of the child from a very different culture with different values, a different language, a different child-rearing style and different family patterns. Such cultural differences may well lead to differences in cognitive style and motivations in children but the principal problem for such children in an alien school is that of a culture clash (Taylor, 1974). Asian and West Indian immigrant groups will tend to experience culture clash; but so, to some extent, will children from stable working-class families. The second category which we might distinguish is *cultural deprivation* properly so-called. Children whose environment does not provide them with important conceptual experiences—for example of pre-school counting, weighing—or of uses of language for labelling concepts and making explicit social contacts; or children, whose play space and material are so restricted that they cannot truly learn through play or who have no toys or play materials, can be regarded as culturally deprived. Such children are liable to suffer from an accumulating developmental lag and a marked unreadiness, sometimes even for the nursery school.

Much more common than either of the other two is what might be called *cultural disorganization*. Many children do not lack stimulation—rather the reverse. The overcrowded home, numerous adults with different ways of interacting with the child and with each other, a multitude of other children, constant television and radio and such like familiar settings provide a richness of stimuli far beyond that of the tranquil "middle class" home. Three aspects of such environments seem to be important from the point of view of cognitive as well as other aspects of development. In such surroundings the child's play is likely to be subject to constant disruption. The adults may themselves be inconsistent in their handling of the child or inconsistent with each other. The child's questions may go unanswered or be answered inconsequentially. Quite apart from cultural differences associated with social class or ethnic differences, such an environment disturbs attention, produces conflictual motivations and disturbs the processes of conceptual growth and structuring upon which cognitive growth depends (Reuchlin and Lézine, 1972).

## Relation to Early Development

A great many research workers have drawn attention to the immense importance of the very early years in the growth of orectic and volitional aspects of personality. In an elaborate synthesis of the results of a great many longitudinal studies, Bloom (Bloom, 1964), comes to the conclusion for example that by the age of four, 50% of the variance of adult intelligence is already there and a further 30% by the age of eight. Of recent years many other pieces of work have been directed to the way in which cognitive and other aspects of psychological growth are structured in the pre-school period. At least from the early work of Piaget onwards to the contemporary ethologists (Richards, 1974), it has been agreed (except by extreme environmentalists) that there are certain predispositions inherent in the child which interact with a provocative milieu. Thus there can be variation from two sources; the child himself and the mainly maternally organized early environment.

Among others, Burton White (1966) has been able to show that differences in competence (intellectual, manipulative, social) arise very early in relation to maternal styles and are well established by the age of three such that children from high competent families are more like highly competent six-year-olds than they are like other three- or six-year-olds. Other writers (for example Reuchlin, Piaget) have stressed the importance of consistency and organization in the early environment, richness and structure in the material which surrounds the child, the differences which result from an open, permissive explanatory style of control permitting the child real choice and one which is authoritarian, non-explanatory and providing forced choices. Bernstein (1971) particularly has drawn attention to linguistic styles or codes, their relationship to socio-cultural groups and to value structures as well as to the balance between verbal and non-verbal forms of communication (Bernstein, 1971).

Finally we should draw attention to the high degree of persistence

(Douglas *et al.*, 1966), in characteristics and the difficulty of changing them in positive ways. This has particular bearing on efforts at "compensatory education". Although there is some evidence that massive interventions involving the whole of the environment can operate to raise functioning even as late as adolescence (Smilansky, 1971), this has only so far proved to be true with groups of the disadvantaged who are higher than the average of their own group. Intervention programmes in the primary school and even in the pre-school with groups of severely disadvantaged children have not been strikingly successful largely it seems because the interventions have been directed to more or less specific aspects of cognitive functioning. The programmes which involve mothers of very young children in a much more global attempt to change the whole climate of early pre-school education seem more likely to succeed (Karnes, 1969; Bloom, 1964; Vasquez and Ouvrey, 1967).

## The School

It does seem to be clear that the origin of most of the differences and inequalities which we observe lies outside the school. Moreover the effects of early education in the family tend to be maintained by the continuing influence of the family throughout the school period. At present it looks as if the role of the school in reducing inequalities is at best very minor. In fact equality of access even to good schools tends to exaggerate differences as the child progresses. If equality of access really means, as it too often does, access to schools which are themselves ranged along a continuum of advantage-disadvantage with the good schools available to the most favoured and the poorer ones to the least, then the fanning out will be the greater.

Nevertheless, schools do make a difference (Wiseman, 1964; Rosenshine, 1971), and probably if we knew how to train teachers and organize for success could perhaps make more. It is also true to say that the extension and improvement of education since the early 1930s although perhaps it has not made much difference to the severely disadvantaged, has in fact provided much increased opportunity of access to secondary and higher education. The proportions—in every country (Riordan, 1973)—of children from working class families in academic and university education are certainly lower than are those from middle class groups: but there has been an increase. Moreover most propagandists overlook the fact that upward social mobility through education tends to spread over more than one generation and to be matched by downward social mobility (De Coster, 1967).

One of the more understandable (but to some extent politically unacceptable) facts about education is that organizational change does not of itself induce other kinds of hoped for change in schools. The same is to some extent also true of changes in pedagogic method or, indeed, of most kinds of innovation. Good examples of this are the work done by the NFER on streaming in primary schools (Lunn, 1966), and the studies by the same organization of reading standards, methods and the like in the county of Kent (Morris, 1966). The streaming enquiry tended to show that such differences as did occur were relatively marginal though they did generally favour non-streaming, particularly where—and this is an important point—the teachers were generally in accord with the educational ideology underlying the notion of heterogeneous groupings. In the Kent enquiries, different methods of teaching reading were examined in a longitudinal way. Broadly it was found that whereas one method, or rather group of methods, seemed to tend to more rapid initial progress, children taught by another group of methods had caught up by the end of the primary school. From this and from other research, what appears more than anything else to distinguish successful learning situations from less successful ones is not so much method or organization but how systematic the teacher is able to be in pursuit of explicit goals, how hopeful the teacher is about children's abilities (Pidgeon, 1970) and how far pupils are enabled to experience success as the result of effort. In a very real sense the problem about streaming is that in practice it often led to lowered expectations on the part of teachers and pupils, to the lower streams having the poorer accommodation, older text-books and in-experienced teachers. Heterogenous groupings present their own problems and do not obligatorily get away from lower expectations for children from poor backgrounds nor do they necessarily contribute to a positive self-image on the part of less able children.

More recently, in face of the fact that differences between pupils are obstinately persistent and tend to be cumulative, American educators particularly have called the whole system of education in primary schools into question. They stress, as others have before them, that "frontal" forms of teaching which involve the whole class in similar learning activities have the disadvantage of inter-individual competitiveness giving the satisfaction of success only to the few at the top and ignoring the fact that an individual might, in comparison with himself, be making quite striking and successful progress (Bloom, 1972). They point out that whatever each individual does, the rank order of the group tends to be stable over many years and to tend towards a self-fulfilling prophecy. Individualized instruction and active participation in learning are at least as old as the Dalton system and there are many variants on the theme—projects, centres of interest, integrated days and so on with little but subjective evidence to go upon as to their efficacy except that, adequately handled by insightful teachers, they are in accord with what we know of children's learning. Moreover all methods from the most rigidly structured to the most open and child centred tend to have their successes and relative failures. What workers like Bloom (1972), Bruner (1971) and Carroll (1963), are advocating is a much more closely structured individual approach which owes its origins to the less mechanistic aspects of neobehaviourism, to theories of motivation based upon reward and to the sorts of analysis of learning sequences which the programmed instruction movement brought to our attention. Bruner suggests, for example, that

> "for any knowledge or empowering skill that exists in the culture there is a corresponding form that is within the grasp of a young learner at the stage of development where one finds him—that any subject can be taught to anybody at any age in some form that is both interesting and honest."

Bloom points out that interest and motivation arise from successful activity; and Kagan and others suggest that what a child is called upon should be thought of in terms of the attainment of clearly defined masteries toward which he can proceed at his own pace getting the reward of absolute success rather than being in a situation where his success is in a comparative-competitive framework.

This rather sketchily outlined thesis is difficult to evaluate in research terms although the model it proposes has been embodied in several attempted new curricula. Learning psychologists would on the whole tend to support it on the ground that it accords with—and indeed so far as Bruner is concerned is derived from the ways in which children learn in "natural" situations whereas much school instruction or teaching not only supposes a competitive and somewhat arbitrary situation but tends to be removed from concretely provocative situations of daily life. It also tends to accord with what was said earlier about the importance of a systematic approach with immediate goals, at least, well-defined in terms that the learner can understand.

## Conclusion

I shall conclude by venturing some opinions about the school as an equalizing or non-equalizing agency. It seems to be clear that, in terms of the great differences in home background and the possible differences in genetic equipment, equal treatment within a system of primary schooling which is essentially normative and largely "frontal" is likely to increase the spread rather than to reduce it—and that this will tend to be true with fundamental skills which are largely cognitive and also with motivational, volitional and attitudinal differences as well. The more normative and competitive a school is, the more clearly will it tend to grade and classify and to socialize children into a hierarchy corresponding to the existing social hierarchy: and this, even though for some children it acts as a promoter of upward social mobility. Recently we have become concerned with sizeable minority groups—immigrant children and children from socio-economic backgrounds which do not fit them well for schools as they are. For these, many local education authorities and schools make a variety of positively discriminatory arrangements—language classes, remedial education, compensatory education, modified curricula and the like—roughly corresponding in conception to the notions which underlay the provision of special classes and schools for children with various handicaps. Some have advocated a revaluation of aspects of content and objectives of primary schools and particularly the dethronement of the primacy of verbal-symbolic thinking since it is in this area that disadvantage is most apparent. In advocating a respect for the home culture of the child where it clashes with the expectations of the schools, there has been a tendency to regard some characteristics of human psychology in learning situations—curiosity, high achievement motivation, delay of gratification and inhibition of impulse, verbal communication, aesthetic awareness and the like—as being class based rather than of value in themselves irrespective of their association with a particularly successful group.

It seems still fair to say that schools as they are, even the best of them, provide an adequate environment for at least half the children they teach and particularly for those who come from stable and on the whole articulate and educated homes. Some perhaps do a good, even an excellent and humane job, for that large minority of children who come from homes which are in one way or another mildly or grossly unsatisfactory or culturally alien. But although schools have changed very considerably in such matters as curricula and general climate of care for their pupils, and although very many attempt to implement the generous notion that all children are valuable in their own right, they do nevertheless grade in various subtle ways which tend to enhance existing differences; nor have we discovered a pedagogic style which enables the school to overcome those out-of-school influences which operate to depress human function.

## References

Bernstein, B. (1971). Social class, language and socialisation. In *Class Codes and*

*Control.* Vol. 1 *Theoretical Studies towards a Sociology of Language.* Edited by B· Bernstein. London: Routledge and Kegan Paul.

Bloom, B. S. (1964). *Stability and Change in Human Characteristics.* New York: Wiley.

Bloom, B. S. (1972). Innocence in education. *School Review,* **80,** 3.

Bruner, J. S. (1971). *The Relevance of Education.* New York: Norton.

Carroll, J. (1963). Model of school learning. *Teachers' College Record,* **64.**

Central Advisory Council for Education. (1967). *Children and their Primary Schools.* Vol. II. The Plowden Report. App. 4. London: HMSO.

Davie, R., Butler, N. and Goldstein, H. (1972). *From Birth to Seven.* London: Longmans.

De Coster, S. (1967). *Essais sur la Régression Sociale Virtuelle et l'Enseignement.* Editions de l'Institut de Sociologie. Brussels: Universite Libre de Bruxelles.

Douglas, J. W. B. (1964). *The Home and the School.* London: MacGibbon and Kee.

Douglas, J. W. B., Kagan, J. and Moss, H. A. (1966). *Birth to Maturity.* New York: Wiley.

Douglas, J. W. B., Ross, J. M. and Simpson, H. R. (1968). *All our Future.* London: Peter Davies.

Kamii, C. K. (1971). Evaluation of learning in pre-school education. In *Handbook on Formative and Summative Evaluation of Student Learning.* Edited by Bloom, B. S., Hastings, J. Thomas and Madaus, George F. New York: McGraw Hill.

Karnes, M. B. (1969). *Investigation of Classroom and at-home Interventions: Research and Development Programme in Pre-School Disadvantaged Children.* Urbana, Illinois: University of Illinois Institute of Research for Exceptional Children.

Lunn, J. C. Barker. (1970). *Streaming in the Primary School.* Slough: NFER.

Morris, J. M. (1966). *Standards and Progress in Reading.* Slough: NFER.

Morris, J. M., Cane, B. and Smithers, J. (1966). *The Roots of Reading.* Slough: NFER.

Peaker, G. F. (1971). *The Plowden Children Four Years Later.* Slough: NFER.

Piaget, J. (1947). *La Psychologie de l'Intelligence.* Paris: Armand Colin.

Pidgeon, D. A. (1970). *Expectation and Pupil Performance.* Slough: NFER.

Reuchlin, M. and Lézine, I. (1972). In *Milieu et Dévéloppement.* Paris: Presses Universitaires de France.

Richards, M. P. M. (Editor) (1974). *The Integration of a Child into a Social World.* London: Cambridge University Press.

Riordan, J. (1973). Survey shows Russians share Western problems. Report on Vasilieva, E. K. Sem'ya i' uschonye uspekhi shkol' nikov. In *Socsiologicheskie Problemy Obrazovaniya i* Vospitaniya. Edited by R. G. Guroya.

Rosenshine, B. (1971). *Teaching Behaviours and Student Achievement.* Slough: NFER.

Smilansky, M. (1971). *Secondary Boarding Schools for Gifted Students from Culturally Disadvantaged Strata.* Technical Report No. 2 Tel. Aviv: Tel Aviv University. Mimeo.

Taylor, F. (1974). *Race, School and Community.* Slough: NFER.

*The Times Higher Educational Supplement.* (1974). 6 September.

Vasquez, A. and Ouvrey, F. (1967). *Vers un Pédagogie Institutionelle.* Paris: François Maspero.

White, L. Burton. (1966). *Child Rearing Practices and the Development of Competence.* Cambridge Massachusetts Laboratory of Human Development. Harvard: Harvard University.

Wiseman, S. (1964). *Education and Environment.* Manchester: Manchester University Press.

Yates, A. G. (1966). *Grouping in Education.* Hamburg: UNESCO Institute for Education.

# The Practice of Education at the Primary Stage

## P. B. RATTENBURY

*Department of Education and Science, London, England*

On a recent visit to inspect Amalgam County Junior School I passed a field full of cows. To my amazement the vast majority of them were standing side by side in a straight line on well worn, well eaten grass gazing at long succulent greenery that lay immediately ahead of them. I stopped fascinated. An occasional cow moved forward munching contentedly, but the vast majority stood their ground.

"Takes 'em some time to get used to it", offered the farmer, trudging past me to his landrover, "Oi've just moved electric fence".

He waved up the field and all was explained by the line of wire cutting off some of the uneaten grass from the cows.

I went on my way pondering on the parable presented to me by these cows; a parable to which I will return shortly. Join me on my visit to Amalgam, a newish school opened about five years ago, brick built, single-storeyed and generally rectilinear in plan. We enter the school and are immediately struck by an excellent central display of children's work in pottery and art. To our right is a pleasantly furnished staff room with fitted carpet and low, easy chairs, but we turn left into a central book and resource area. Once again the display catches the eye and the furnishing is pleasant, modern, functional and in scale for children. These features are constantly brought to our notice as we progress round the school and it is very apparent that great care has been given to the selection of furniture, wall and floor finishes, and that this care has been mirrored by the staff and the children's attitude to presentation and display.

The books and audio-visual resources at this central point are interesting both in their positioning and variety. Fiction and non-fiction appear in roughly equal numbers and the latter selection contains, in addition to a large range of books specifically produced for children, a fair selection of first class adult reference material. The audio-visual resources include a portable television, a number of portable tape recorders and some slide viewers. The very pleasant lady, who is issuing both books and equipment to children, introduces herself during a break in activities as a parent. She points out a lock-up store, where the majority of expensive equipment is housed, and assures us that we will find smaller equipment stores and book displays scattered around the general teaching areas. Throughout our conversation a steady trickle of children have been using the books, some to check a point, others signing them out to take away and yet others settling down to work with them, or equipment at the nearby tables.

A door opens, and we hear the strains of an orchestra hard at work, rehearsing in an adjoining but acoustically isolated music room. We turn away to the left and find ourselves in the general teaching area. This is a mixture of spaces which include one large room about the size of a traditional classroom, another space about twice this size and a small room of about 200 sq. ft in area. In the traditional classroom the furniture is arranged in an informal fashion so that the thirty-four children in the space are working in groups of four, five or six. The teacher is moving between groups and it is soon apparent that, though the main concentration of effort is on the three Rs, the groups are busy at different activities. They answer our questions readily and confidently and do not appear to be in the slightest bit discomforted by the presence of two strange adults.

In the larger space we notice one of the small book areas, that the librarian had mentioned, and we see children working on their own as well as in groups, some using the various mechanical aids. One group is kneeling on the floor, working on a huge painting; we almost stumble across another group struggling to work out a tricky mathematical problem. Various practical bays enable children to develop skills and interests, here a science experiment, there cookery or needlework. Boys and girls are no longer restricted to the particular crafts once deemed suitable for their sex. A display corner has been set up to focus attention and work on historical and geographical material. Our eye is particularly caught by a superb model of a viking ship, which we will meet again later in the visit.

We make for the small group room and discover two children making music, while two more perfect a puppet play. Some sixty or seventy children occupy the large area and two teachers move among them responding to their needs. We move on to another general teaching area, similarly organized, past two courtyards, one of which contains pets in hutches while the other boasts fish in an ornamental pool and green living plants. Both courts bring light and air and the outside world into the heart of education. In this second general teaching area the small group room is being used for a French lesson, while the rest of the area contains a mix of activities, much as we previously observed, though somewhat differently organized. One teacher is obviously helping a small group who are finding academic work difficult, while another appears to be telling her children a story.

We follow a group of thirty children out of the general teaching area, past the music room which now seems to be occupied by actors, to the assembly hall. Within moments groups of children are working on apparatus. Half an hour later the teacher claps her hands and the children dismantle the equipment, carrying, wheeling and pushing it back into place before leaving the room. Another group appear; a record player is switched on; the mood changes and concentration on intricate, graceful movement becomes all important.

A bell rings, the first we have heard all morning, and the children go out for a break. We follow them to the large playground where traditional ball games get under way; to a wild copse which they appear to be destroying with a game of cops and robbers; and to a play court broken by small walls where individual and small private games develop. As it is sunny, we stay outside for a few minutes when the children are called in, and then we notice that some of them are back using the environment to investigate, to make music, to do noisy craft work or just to sit and read. A large group of children emerge with a teacher. A small boy is proudly carrying the viking ship. We follow them to a local pond and share their excitement at the successful launch.

Another day, another visit and the activities would have changed, the grouping of children would have altered, the teachers would be differently disposed but the general air of purposeful activity would remain. The children would be able to tell you about what they are doing, and the teachers would be able to tell you where that activity fitted into the child's general pattern of development. As its name implies, Amalgam County Junior is a creation of the mind but it is not all that fanciful. The ground plan of the school exists and building starts next year. Every individual activity I have described is taking place in primary schools around the country. Some would fit this description very closely and many are working towards some such organization.

I took you round Amalgam School because I wanted to show you what teachers are trying to achieve in practice in education at the primary stage. Let us return for a moment to my cow field, for in many ways these animals highlight the difficulties we all face in an era of change. The wire fence was down and the cows did not know how to react. Traditions and restrictions impinge upon us and we often have difficulty in determining how we should act. Primary teachers, just like the rest of us, see restrictions being cleared from their way, the pasture is green and tempting but the resultant freedom causes its own complications.

The most immediately apparent freedom stems from the gradual demise of the 11+ examination, though some form of selection procedure for allocating schools or streams in secondary education is still retained by about half the education authorities in England. The lessening of the bonds imposed by this examination is considered by some to be responsible for a supposed fall in standards. It may indeed be true that the specific English, Mathematics and so-called Intelligence exercises tested by this method are no longer so competently performed. Other things being equal the successful schools were generally those that specifically coached for these tests. These results were achieved by repetition and familiarization in the same fashion that an addict may become adept at *The Times* crossword while still having difficulty with the *Daily Telegraph* and vice versa. Another well publicized restriction has been the number of children with which a single teacher has had to deal.

Numbers of themselves are not necessarily too demanding of teachers but allied to crowding, they can be very restrictive. In the late 1950s and early 1960s space requirements in primary schools appeared to be improving but the inflation in building costs and the relative reduction in educational expenditure has lost the ground that was being gained. The least space-taking organization is for all children to concentrate on book-learning all day in desks. All that we have learnt about children and their learning needs, from the time of Froebel on, argues for a variety of activities. We need more, not less, space and its lack can place great restrictions even on the most imaginative teachers.

Among the most restrictive features in education are the in-built attitudes of educationalists and parents. Old methods only require repetition, new methods require imagination. Throughout the last thirty-five years English education has been short on imagination. In many of our activities research has shown quite clearly that we should be involving children in learning processes. We see the fence has been moved but it is simpler to teach the calves to munch the grass in the way we were taught to munch it yesterday.

Throughout the last hundred years there have been two clearly defined movements in education. The first is the more obvious. There has been more of it. Increasing numbers of children and the increasing age range has seen to that. In the primary field, in the last ten years, the introduction of middle schools, for about 10–12% of children in the relevant age groups, and the present expansion of nursery education both require a re-examination of attitudes and an adaptation of techniques by all concerned with the younger children. The second trend is in many ways the more challenging for the teacher; it is the steady move towards more individual treatment of each child. The organization of work in a way that assumes that the children in the class are all at the same point in learning, though still frequently practised, is recognized by most teachers of primary children to be an expedient rather than the ideal, an expedient that is practised on occasions by the best teachers to enable them to concentrate their efforts on a few of the individuals in their control. I often feel that the primary teacher is in the position advocated as the ideal by Rousseau— the all-wise tutor, for the individual child. The successful teacher is the one who, despite two enormous handicaps manages the nearest approach to this ideal. The two handicaps are that all-wise people are few and far between and that our tutor has to deal with between thirty and forty individuals.

How then is the attempt to approach this ideal, however unsteadily, ever begun? Despite all rumours to the contrary the concentration remains firmly based on the three Rs. Without some capability in these any success for later individual learning must be severely restricted. This concentration is often obscured by the lurching changes of fashion which can take a sensible reform to a logical extreme of absurdity. The fashions affect the educational scene, as they do the world of haute couture, in ways that make it very difficult to predict, while one is in the period of change, which facet will last and which prove ephemeral. Who for example would have hazarded that the most ridiculous and useless of all pieces of Victorian male attire would last hundred years and more—I refer to the necktie. The current educational fashions attract much attention and give rise to arguments often conducted in jargon terms which, satisfactorily for the prolongation of argument, mean something different to each party to the discussion. Unfortunately the fashions are most easily listed by their jargon terms—open-plan, team-teaching, the integrated day, mixed ability and vertical grouping. Each arrangement referred to has developed in some measure, I suspect as an attempt to approach the ideal of treating each child as an individual despite a teacher–pupil ratio which denies this aim.

The open plan development of the moment exactly demonstrates my thesis. A predecessor of mine was giving talks to teachers in 1870; in-service training is at least that old. His slides show an open plan school with organizational diagrams describing the arrangement of monitorial groups. Early photographs of classrooms in single teacher schools show the use of curtains as staffing improved. Curtains were replaced by partitions as the improved staffing became permanent and then the partitions hardened into walls. The box classroom lasted for fifty years or more before it was felt to be repressive. Teachers wished to co-operate for the benefit of the children. Some activities demanded smaller groupings, the doors came off, the partitions came down and in some instances this was formalized into large rectangular, open-plan spaces. Hopefully we are now settling for delineation according to the type of activity, to the various group sizes; providing open areas shared by an appropriate number of children and teachers, a number which will not be out of scale with the age and working patterns of the children concerned.

The use of shared spaces has developed with the concept of co-operation between teachers for the benefit of the children; co-operation that has had, in many schools, to replace competition between the staff. This worthwhile co-operation is possible, though more difficult, when operating in separate classrooms off corridors and much more difficult when schools are expanded into hutted encampments. It has been formalized into the concept of team-teaching by groups of two, three, four or more teachers. Sometimes the arrangement amounts to little more than specialist teaching at a very early age, a practice which, at that stage has some important disadvantages.

It has long been the fashion to reject all but the most rudimentary forms of central timetabling for children under eleven, leaving the organization to the individual teacher operating in her individual classroom. When teachers co-operate a greater degree of organization becomes necessary, whether achieved by central or group imposition, or whether arrived at by a continuing dialogue between the teachers concerned. At its best this co-operation leads teachers to test their ideas and refine their approaches in a continually evolving analysis with like-minded professional colleagues; at its worst it can degenerate into a sharing out of activities between teachers for their own convenience rather than for the benefit of the children. The teaching team needs to be closer to the present developments in football, where it is often difficult to distinguish positions on the field but where each player is contributing to the team effort, than to cricket—a series of individual activities masquerading under the title of a team game. To take the football analogy a step further the headmaster/goalkeeper, often the only distinguishable member of the team, is keenly interested in all that is taking place and is very much involved at moments of crisis.

He constantly stimulates his team by rolling, throwing or kicking the ball to the most appropriate team mate. Teachers as a body have yet to develop the team philosophy to its limits, but, where experiments have been pursued, some very interesting developments have occurred. The variety of potential contact between teacher and learner provides far more chances for manoeuvre if three adults are dealing with a hundred pupils rather than one with thirty-three. Some degree of openness in planning is essential if teachers are to explore the possibilities of cooperation.

Another phrase much in vogue is the "integrated day". I can never think of the term without being reminded of the *Punch* cartoon of the small girl walking home hand in hand with her mother. "And what did you do at school?" she is asked. "I disintegrated the day" comes the fiendish reply. I have often felt like doing the same thing myself.

The integrated day is, in essence, an organizational response to the ideal of teaching each child as an individual. It is immediately apparent that individual children's needs and response are different and thus it can quickly be appreciated that children's time requirements for specific activities will vary. The traditional approach is to assume an average child and arrange a balanced timetable for him. Whether the latter is organized by the Head or the class teacher is immaterial. Once arranged all the children in the group will work at the same activity at the same time and for the same amount of time. Very few parents would arrange their families' lives like this and increasing numbers of teachers are dissatisfied with this approach. The ideal would be for each child to follow the prescribed activities for the length of time most appropriate to her own learning processes. In practice there is a tendency for the class to break into groups each of which can be following separate paths. The skilful primary teacher organizes the activities so that she is able to teach, help and encourage where this is necessary and at the same time supervise less demanding activities. For example in Amalgam School we saw a group of six children painting, another group reading, another group researching or writing up a project, a further group engaged in creative writing, while the rest were doing mathematics. Half of the mathematicians were working at previously organized problems while the remainder were being introduced to some new topic. It would be this final group that would at that moment, be engaging the teacher's attention. Obviously this is only an approach to the ideal but it is an approach that enables the individuals' problems to be more closely studied and dealt with. A few schools have gone far beyond this arrangement following the doctrine of child-centred education close to the logical absurdity of child-organized education. Teachers stand aside and watch children learn from experience. This the children do if the teachers are incredibly gifted, but they can all too easily waste their time, if the teachers are not.

A large portion of early learning is connected with the conventions that a particular nation has developed over many centuries. Our current forms of speech, reading, spelling, and arithmetic could not be learnt by a child in a vacuum. A child locked in a room with a large number of pennies and a large number of pound notes could never work out how many of one equalled one of the other, especially if his elders and betters decided to change the answer from 240 to 100 on a pre-determined day. Certain conventions have to be taught and teachers have a duty to teach them. They also have a duty to introduce children to the skills that they will require in modern society and practice will be necessary to entrench these. Everything else teachers attempt to do is pure gain for society, which generally undervalues their efforts. Attitudes, responses, interaction of the individual with the group, all have to be caught rather than taught and the school is often positing ideal inter-personal and community solutions which are being rejected by those adults who the children meet outside school.

Two more terms which are frequently aired in discussions of modern primary practice are both connected with the grouping of children. Both have developed in response to the recognition of the individuality of each child and have been made possible by the improvement in teacher–pupil ratio. Taken together they can, in organizational terms, appear to set the clock back a hundred years to the smaller board school. Here the teacher struggled to cope with a large number of children of mixed ages, spanning the complete ability range. The two terms to which I refer, mixed ability and family grouping, may appear at first sight to refer to an organizational arrangement of the same order. "Mixed ability" refers to the organization of children into classes each containing the full academic ability span encountered in ordinary schools. This may be done within a year group, or across two year groups or even the whole age range of the school. Where the mix includes more than one year group it is referred to as "vertical" or "family grouping".

These developments made workable by improved staffing ratios were occasioned by some teachers, dissatisfaction with the existing system of rigid grouping by ability and chronological age. Yet those developments, in themselves, were a step towards dealing with the child as an individual. Any teacher facing a group, however carefully selected, however carefully creamed off, is all too soon made aware of the differences of pace, response and progress. University teachers, who only see the academic cream, are well able to appreciate these phenomena which soon became apparent to the most junior primary teachers whose children's range of ability will almost certainly be wider than that of university entrants. Similarly all recent medical evidence demonstrates the fallibility of the birth date as an accurate guide to a child's physical or academic maturity. The ending of either or both forms of organizing the grouping of children has some dis-advantages, especially if imposed on teachers who believe in their efficacy, but it does have the great advantage of underlining the individuality of each child.

A seven- and an eleven-year-old may have identical academic aptitudes and performance but teachers are unlikely to treat them identically. Two nine-year-olds, one with the spread of aptitude and performance of a seven-year-old and the other of an eleven-year-old, will too often be treated as though their problems were identical. In the same way to cope adequately with two children of the same age, one of whom can just cope with the recognition aspects of reading while the other is devouring books well beyond her years, concentrates the minds of some teachers wonderfully, even if it bemuses others.

Research into linguistics has highlighted the academic deprivation experienced by those whose pre-school language experience is limited, either by lack of contact with adults or by lack of spoken language in a given environment. This research is now being acted on in the pre-school years both here and in other countries. The growth of nursery education, the increase of play groups, television publicity and programmes, all should help to increase public awareness and, more importantly, to increase language interaction between children and adults. In Russia grandmothers are joining nursery classes just to talk with the children. A real concentration of effort at this end of the educational scale might far outweigh the success gained by our traditional concentration of effort at secondary and university levels. There is good reason to suppose that some children arrive at school with too little language to make use of early school experiences. Our schooling methods are organized by the linguistically more able and benefit the linguistically more able.

The linguistic gap may be reinforced by the expectations of the many people connected with a particular child. The power of expectation to reverse this trend has also been demonstrated. If teacher and school, parent and society combine to influence a child, that child's self-expectation can often be dramatically increased with a consequent improvement in both self-awareness and academic results.

The attempt to develop each individual child to his or her individual socially-acceptable potential is one of the two main aims of any society's educational system. The other, and equally important, is concerned with its own strengthening and constant re-creation. As long as society is relatively secure, static or totalitarian in concept, this second aim is fairly easy to direct and manipulate. Our predecessors knew what they desired of education. Now that we are in a time of change old standards are less applicable. The children now in primary schools will be my age in 2010. Which of us could forecast what life holds in store for them. I can only hazard that it will be different. Adults may need to be more adaptable, they may well need every skill of mind or hand that we can put at their disposal. In this era of change it seems to me that the concentration on the individual in primary schools has been wholly advisable. This concentration must never be at the expense of that particular child's social needs at the time and in the environment in which he or she is living. The parents or the community may be pressing demands on the child which the teacher will ignore at his peril. To make certain that the social demands are not unreasonable it behoves society to appreciate just what education at the primary stage is attempting to achieve. Because children in primary schools no longer do what we did at their age, do not know the capital of Peru or cannot chant their twelve times table; because secretaries it is said can no longer spell as well as their mothers did (it is interesting to reflect that those mothers' daughters may now be at university); the educational system in general and the primary schools in particular come under attack. There is no firm evidence that there has been a drop in standards, there are even indications to the contrary. For example more students are getting better A-levels than ever before. Professor Bernard Lovell was recently quoted in the national press as saying that students of the last ten years were better than their predecessors. Others may not agree! Schools are sitting targets and what sportsman can resist. No teacher can prove that what she is doing is beneficial for a particular child and any parent can find evidence of poor spelling, an incorrect sum or bad behaviour. In my view, the improvement in general educational standards over the thirty-two years since I first faced a class is both enormous and incontrovertible. True, factual knowledge may not be taken aboard by rote, formal English exercise may be plunging towards a timely grave, books full of repetitive arithmetic problems may no longer fill our locker desks but look at what we have gained in their place.

Let me take you back to Amalgam County Junior and refresh your memory by listing what we saw in addition to the varied work to strengthen the three Rs. There was music, dance and drama. Physical education ranged from free expression to controlled movement. Art and craft flourished and great care was given to display and presentation. Inquiring minds were investigating the environment and working on scientific observation and experiments. French was being taught and spoken by young children. Books were in evidence and in use. Complicated equipment was being handled by the same young children.

All these are solid advances most of which can be seen in primary schools up and down the country. Yet it is all too easy for such activities to develop stereotypes just as their predecessors did. Text books may be replaced by equally inappropriate work cards, copy books may have disappeared but mindless copying disguised as topic work can all too easily take its place. Chanting by rote may have been eliminated from mathematics to reappear as the dominant approach in French. As long as the individual child and his needs remain high in the list of teacher's priorities these replacements will be exposed for shams or revealed as strengths.

Major battles have to be won in hearts as well as in the minds of teachers and parents. It is all very well for us to realize the primacy of spoken rather than written English. It is far more difficult to turn this realization into practice and then convince adults brought up to a different practice that our new approach has long term academic merit. Reading is as vital for pleasure as for factual content, expanding the imagination is more important than increasing the store of factual knowledge. These are vital concepts, I believe, for the whole of primary education but concepts that disturb many adults who believe that children's noses should be kept to the grindstone. For sharpening steel, grindstones have their uses, for imaginative noses they can be very destructive.

These and other battles yet to be appreciated, are there to be fought and won. The climate is right, for the enormous step forward of the last thirty years in primary education will be hard to eradicate. Children are people and teachers are respecting their individuality. I am full of hope for the next thirty years. If my opening parable is applicable, I must report that, as I passed that field on my way back home, the cows had moved into the fresh grass and were munching with relish, and I suspect increased nourishment.

# Making Adults More Equal: The Scope and Limitations of Public Educational Policy

## JEAN FLOUD

*Newnham College, Cambridge, England*

In a recent lecture to the British Academy Professor James Meade discussed the inheritance of inequality (Meade, 1973). He pointed out that:

> "In a society in which there were no governmental interference with the operation of the competitive markets and no other artificial impediments to competition or mobility, persons who were similarly endowed would tend to receive the same incomes, but as individual citizens are not equally endowed, then personal incomes may continue to be unequal, even in a fully competitive laissez-faire society with unrestricted mobility".

Of course, we do not live in such a society; but the real world is too complicated to understand without the aid of abstractions and Professor Meade devoted his lecture to a theoretical consideration of the four principal factors which commonsense suggests would cause individuals to be unequally endowed; namely, genes, property, education and social contacts. These are the elements of family background or class position which determine people's economic and social opportunities—their "life chances"—and Professor Meade refers to them as *structured* elements of good or bad *fortune*, distinguishing them from the *chance* elements of good or bad *luck*, which are responsible for the divergent fates even of persons of similar fortune. With beautiful lucidity he expounds the intricate relationships determining the transmission of the elements of fortune, showing how they are all interrelated in a complicated single system—a biological–demographic–social–economic system—of which it is extremely difficult to get at the separate elements in order to measure their relative importance. His theoretical exercise has to be understood as a practical preliminary to further, more sophisticated, empirical work by economists and sociologists who share his view that, if we want to reduce social inequalities, we must make changes in our institutions which will have the effect of readjusting this underlying system of inherited inequalities.

Just about one year before Professor Meade delivered his lecture, the American sociologist Christopher Jencks with a number of Harvard colleagues published a book called *Inequality: A Reassessment of the Effect of Family and Schooling in America* (Jencks, *et al.*, 1972). Professor Jencks, like Professor Meade, distinguishes "luck" from "fortune", only to claim, however, that what he calls luck is immensely more important than fortune (that is to say, than family and schooling, the elements of inherited class position) in the determination of social inequalities in America today. This is a disturbing claim, as Professor Meade acknowledges at the end of his lecture. As I have explained, he himself has undertaken a theoretical exercise in abstraction, designed to elucidate the interrelationship of the inherited factors which seem to be fundamentally responsible for the persistence of social inequalities. Professor Jencks, on the other hand, has undertaken a concrete, statistical exercise in order to answer an empirical question: how far can inequalities of income in the United States today be accounted for by the inequalities of social and educational opportunity which have been established by social scientists over the past thirty years or so? He claims to show that they cannot be so explained, which seems to make Professor Meade's exercise unnecessary, as well as to carry very far-reaching implications for the design of policies if we want to reduce inequalities. For if Professor Jencks is right, and if there are no features or developments peculiar to American society to account for his findings, we may be inclined to conclude that in no advanced industrial society can social inequalities be reduced by means of an attack on the system of inherited inequalities through educational, social and economic reform; instead, we must rely on a continuing day-to-day war on the economic inequalities which the chances of luck are continually re-establishing; we must turn from educational expansion and reform, for example, to devising schemes of income insurance designed to neutralize the effects of luck in the labour market; we must see to it that in every generation the lucky subsidise the unlucky and that the link between vocational success and living standards is effectively broken.

Professor Meade suspends judgement on this new issue in the debate on the sources of inequality, but is inclined to stick to his view that structure is crucial and that the fundamental attack must be on fortune rather than luck. I should like to use the occasion of this meeting to contribute briefly to the further discussion for which the topic evidently calls; but of course, as the occasion demands, I shall confine myself, among the elements of fortune, to education. This, however, is not a matter for regret; for though education is only one of the elements of fortune or class position singled out by Professors Meade and Jencks, it is the one on which the highest hopes of reformers have been pinned and on which public policy has concentrated most heavily. How vulnerable is it to the suggestion that these hopes are misplaced?

It is often said nowadays that, as a matter of fact, educational opportunities cannot be equalized unless society is already fairly equal, since parents cannot be prevented from handing on their privileges and handicaps in large measure to their children. This amounts to a proposition about the way in which the elements of fortune in Professor Meade's complex system interact with each other. It states in effect that education, which is of course itself one of the elements in the system, always produces what Professor Meade calls positive feedback and never negative feedback; that is to say, that as a rule it reinforces and rarely counteracts the effects of the other elements in the system (genes, property, social contacts). This brings us to the heart of our problem, since Professor Jencks subscribes to this proposition and offers it in one form or another as the fundamental explanation of his empirical findings, which are to the effect that the massive post-war expenditures of public money on education in America have not been accompanied by any modification of the prevailing pattern of economic inequality, and that differences in individual incomes in America cannot be explained by differences in educational opportunity. Education does not make adults more equal, he insists, and this is because, as he puts it, schools do not "change" people. If they did change people (i.e. endow them with scarce skills), those with more education, or different kinds of education, would have incomes which would vary accordingly; and the larger the educational budget, the more equal would be the distribution of income. But this he shows is not so.

The expansion and more equal distribution of educational opportunities since 1945 in America has not had the "expected" economic effects; certainly not on the distribution of earnings and possibly not on productivity either. Pre-tax earnings have become somewhat more unequal and though the level of earnings generally has risen, it may not have done so at the same rate as the proportion of highly educated persons in the labour force. If it were true that education provided people with marketable skills which are in short supply, these trends would represent a paradox. Moreover, although he finds that variations in the number of years of formal education and in the credentials thus acquired go a long way to explain the variations in individual occupational achievements, they do little or nothing to explain variations in individual incomes. For incomes are widely dispersed about the means of those earned in the different occupations and Professor Jencks makes the point that:

> "to bring everyone's income closer to the average for the occupation in which he finds himself would do more to reduce inequality overall than to bring the occupational averages closer together".

Job opportunity and the acquisition on the job of rather specific social and intellectual skills, rather than educational opportunity and occupational achievement, is what accounts for variations in individual incomes; and job opportunity is the name for a kind of luck, the outcome of an incalculable miscellany of chance skills, circumstances and events. The tightening bond between education and occupation is thus shown to be spurious; education provides credentials, not skills; it is an epiphenomenon, standing in relation to economic success and failure as a fever stands to sickness and health; that is to say, as an accompanying symptom, not as an explanatory variable.

The issues are exceedingly complex and much of the necessary discussion could only be profitably conducted by economists and statisticians. Nevertheless, since the rationale of public policy in the field of education is in question it is worth asking ourselves how surprised we ought to be by Professor Jencks's findings? For only if we are very surprised by his findings need we entertain his conclusions. He writes, for example:

> "Variations in what children learn are largely dependent on what they bring to school, not on variations in what the schools offer them. Publicly maintained schools are more alike than parents and teachers think they are.

> "If everyone had the same amount of schooling, the differences between people who now drop out and those who stay would be the same; dropouts and stayers are kinds of people, the differences between which are not attributable to their being less or more educated; there are important differences between the more and the less educated but the schools are not responsible for these differences.

> "Neither the overall level of educational resources nor any specific easily

identifiable school policy has much effect on the test scores or educational attainment of students who start out at a disadvantage.

"Educational compensation is usually of marginal value to the recipients."

These are neither theoretical propositions nor empirical statements; they are conjectural half-truths. Must we accept them in order to explain the findings that providing free secondary and higher education on a large scale for nearly thirty years has not had an equalizing effect on the distribution of incomes in America, and that the relative incomes of American citizens A and B have very little to do with their relative educational experiences and attainments? I do not think so.

I will not dwell on the former finding, except to point out the practical limitations of summary measures of inequality in the distribution of incomes (e.g. the Gini Coefficient, or the Coefficient of Variation used by Professor Jencks) as criteria for evaluating particular social policies such as educational expansion and reform. I have the impression (as a layman, of course) that a large body of theoretical and comparative inquiries into the distribution of original incomes (i.e. incomes before taxes and benefits have made their impact) have as their most substantial general outcome that such measures of overall distribution present the end result of a complex set of interrelationships between factors of very different social, economic and political significance and so by their nature, are blunt instruments for the evaluation of particular social policies. These measures are notoriously constant over long periods, masking changes in the relative position of social groups which offset each other, and they do not distinguish between economies at very different stages of development (though it makes a difference whether one is low-paid in a wealthy or a poor society, and whether one is in the social condition of poverty and not merely low-paid—i.e. at the tail end of a statistical distribution of incomes).

I do want, however, to dwell on the second finding, that differences of educational opportunity do not explain much of the variation in individual incomes. Measures of the independent influence of educational opportunity on people's life-chance give different results according to what you mean by "education"—technically speaking, how you construct the variable "education" for the purpose of your measuring exercise. Now in Professor Meade's theoretical model, grounded as it is in common-sense, the element of fortune called "education" is defined very broadly to include practically all the environmental influences affecting an individual's character, motivation and skills. It is arguable whether his model might not be improved by the introduction of a distinction between the diffuse and informally transmitted influences of family upbringing and the formally transmitted intellectual and professional skills for which other institutions are specifically and characteristically responsible. I am myself inclined to think that it would; and so at first glance, it looks as though Professor Jencks has the advantage, since he does make use of a distinction between what he terms the "cognitive skills" and "non-cognitive traits" possessed by individuals. Unfortunately, one can measure the former but not the latter and this fact is Professor Jencks's undoing.

Whereas in Professor Meade's model "luck" is the opposite of "fortune", which is to say, it represents the random differences of personal circumstance (as against the structured differences of class position) which are responsible for inequalities of social condition, Professor Jencks's categories of luck and fortune rest upon no such logical distinction. They are empirical categories; luck is what cannot be specified and measured, the residual miscellany or ragbag of factors which are either unspecifiable or unmeasurable, or both. Non-cognitive traits happen to be unmeasurable and are therefore buried in this residual miscellany of factors called "luck"; but it is plainly false to infer that because they are unmeasurable they are therefore unstructured in Professor Meade's sense—i.e. governed in their incidence by the randomness of chance or "luck".

For my part, I would eschew the concept of luck in discussing social inequalities—it is a term of ordinary parlance which is laden with meanings which are irrelevant and misleading in discussions about social inequalities. But as used by Professor Meade it is perfectly defensible; as used by Professor Jencks, on the other hand, it is indefensible, embodying as it does a confusion between two separate distinctions: on the one hand, the distinction between structured inequalities of class position and random differences of personal circumstance; on the other hand, the distinction between measurable and unmeasurable social inequalities and individual differences. This confusion is responsible for Professor Jencks's quite unwarranted conclusions about the inefficacy of schooling and the irrelevance of education to inequalities of means among adults.

Professor Jencks's conclusions are unwarranted by his empirical findings, which include no measure of the diffuse educational effects of schooling which he wrongly supposes to be purely a matter of chance. In the ragbag of unspecified differences between individuals which together account for half of the variation in their incomes are the so-called "non-cognitive traits", by which Professor Jencks explains that he means personality differences that are believed to make for economic success and which social scientists have spent much time trying to capture with the aid of concepts like "need achievement", "the Protestant Ethic" and "future orientation". He acknowledges that their influence is considerable, and may even be greater than that of factors which do lend themselves to measurement. But he discusses them only very briefly because "we do not even have generally agreed upon names for these traits much less a system for measuring them".

Parents and teachers, of course, set much store by these non-cognitive traits and believe that they are inculcated by schools as well as families. They do not doubt that there are "good" and "bad" homes and schools and that good schools can help offset bad homes and that bad schools can undo the work of good homes and vice versa. Professor Jencks is certain that they are mistaken about schools because his measures of differences in the quality of schools do not help significantly to explain differences in educational outcomes and inequalities of earnings among adults. He measures school quality in terms of financial resources, and takes social and racial composition and curriculum into account by analysing their effects on test performance, which he in turn relates to income differences. He explains that he has ignored differences in the internal life of schools and in the attitudes and values they inculcate. Why, then, is he so sure that schools are more alike than parents and teachers think? He has concentrated, he says, on the *effects* of schooling and especially on effects that might be expected to persist into adulthood. He thus seems to deny non-cognitive traits the status of educational *effects*; but actually, his difficulty is that "we do not know what these non-cognitive effects (of schooling) are likely to be" and we do not know how to specify and measure them.

By the same token, however, we do not know either, what the non-cognitive effects of family upbringing are likely to be. In this case, however, Professor Jencks approaches the problem indirectly by constructing a comprehensive variable termed "family background" to which he was able to give a value in his path analysis of the determinants of individual achievement. By this means he avoids the need to assign them to the ragbag called "luck".

"Family background" is an ingenious measure of the homogeneity of a child's social environment in the family, covering the economic status and education of parents, family size, parental interest in education, attitudes towards achievement and neighbourhood characteristics. It is an hypothetical variable which cannot be measured directly but can be inferred by looking at the average effects of growing up in a family on all the children who did so. It is a weighted combination of all the non-genetic characteristics that make siblings alike. Of course, it is not a unitary concept with a consistent meaning in all contexts and it exercises its influence differently on different outcomes of exposure to it (for example, on cognitive skills and non-cognitive traits); but it by-passes the problem of unmeasured features of home environment and emerges as significantly related to individual differences in cognitive skills, amount of education, educational attainments, occupational achievements and even, moderately so, to differences in individual incomes. Supposing that an analogous, comprehensive measure of school background were constructed and set against this measure of Family Background—would it not provide a means of testing what might be termed the countervailing potential of a child's schooling? Other things being equal, the hypothesis would run, the greater the discrepancies in children's family and school background and the longer the period of their exposure to schooling, the more would the hypothetical variable contribute to the explanation of income differences among adults.

"Family Background" is an empirically derived, indirect expression of the association and interaction of all the elements in Professor Meade's theoretical system of inherited inequalities, except genetically determined ability and education provided outside the home. Professor Jencks's measure of the influence of education outside the home is defective, as we have seen, in being limited to its quantifiable effects on cognitive skills and formal attainments. It seems possible that an improved analysis could yield a more positive and plausible picture of the influence of educational opportunities on earnings, even allowing for the weakening effects of chance on the connection (i.e. Professor Meade's "luck") as well as of all the factors extraneous to inequalities of class position which determine relative incomes (all the scarcities and rigidities of supply and demand and the interventions of government which Professor Meade simplifies away in the assumptions built into his model).

We do not need to accept Professor Jencks's view of education as ineffectual and irrelevant simply on the ground that it is a necessary postulate to account for his findings, for these derive from an analysis which is logically flawed and empirically deficient. If it is true that schools do not change people, it must be true in its own right, as it were. Professor Jencks's conclusions are unwarranted; it is of course, another question whether they are true—but that is a matter for another kind of investigation altogether, and for another lecture. Reserving judgement meanwhile, let us follow the argument further.

Disillusioned by his findings, Professor Jencks concludes that schools do not change people and invites us, in thinking about schools, to abandon what he calls the "factory" metaphor for a "family" metaphor.

The idea seems to be that since we do not think of families as institutions that change people, or demand of them that they should do so, to think of schools as families would lead us to look at schooling as an end in itself rather than as a means to some other end and that this will yield a fresh rationale for public expenditure on education. The idea is intuitively attractive but it does not withstand closer scrutiny. Considering education as an end in itself turns out to mean denying its special claim on public funds, which is assumed to rest upon a belief in its economic potency.

> "There is no evidence that building a school playground, for example, will affect the students' chances of learning to read, getting into college, or making $50,000 a year when they are 50. Building a playground may, however, have a considerable effect on the students' chances of having a good time during recess when they are 8. The same thing is probably also true of small classes, competent teachers, and a dozen other things that distinguish adequately from inadequately financed schools.

> "Adequate school funding cannot, then, be justified on the grounds that it makes life better in the hereafter. But it can be justified on the grounds that it makes life better right now. This suggests that students' and teachers' claims on the public purse are no more legitimate than the claims of highway users who want to get home a few minutes faster, manufacturers of supersonic aircraft who want to help their stockholders pay for Caribbean vacations, or medical researchers who hope to extend a man's life expectancy by another year or two. But neither are the schools' claims any less legitimate than the claims of other groups."

The analogy with the family rather than the factory means providing for diversity of schooling to match the diversity of family life and freedom of choice for parents and children:

> "The ideal system is one that provides as many varieties of schooling as its children and parents want and finds ways of matching children to schools that suit them. Since the character of an individual's schooling appears to have relatively little long-term effect on his development, society as a whole rarely has a compelling interest in limiting the range of educational choices open to parents and students. Likewise, since professional educators do not seem to understand the long-term effects of schooling any better than parents do, there is no compelling reason why the profession should be empowered to rule out alternatives that appeal to parents, even if they seem educationally 'unsound'."

and also, paying for what you want in the way of education after the eighth or ninth grade (by which time you will have exhausted your claim to equality of opportunity and free education at public expense, since as Professor Jencks shows, you will already have acquired such cognitive skills as will make a measurable difference to your capacity to earn a living in adulthood).

Something has gone wrong with the argument. Professor Jencks is saying that if public expenditure on education does not make for more equal earnings, it is irrelevant to the problem of securing social justice and must be defended on quite other grounds. I leave aside the difficulty with the family metaphor, that public expenditure on family support programmes do not pretend to equalize earnings, and are judged as contributions to the alleviation of social injustice—which would seem to entail judging educational expenditure in the same terms. More fundamental than this gap in the argument seems to be a misunderstanding about the relations of equality and social justice.

Arguments about social justice (Honoré, 1970) are about claims and entitlements to the perquisites of well-being (life; health; nourishment; shelter; clothing; space; opportunities for acquiring knowledge and skill; for participation in decision making; recreation, travel etc.). In principle, everyone can claim an equal share of these resources simply in virtue of being human; but there are principles of rational dis-crimination (e.g. need, desert, choice) which modify this basic equality of claims and it is difficult to envisage a social situation in which the demands of social justice would be met by an equal distribution of all these necessities and amenities. Professor Meade is speaking directly to this problem of just claims and entitlements, since inherited inequalities discriminate irrationally (i.e. without reference to needs or desert or choice) between persons who, in principle, can claim equal shares of available necessities and amenities: the endowments of fortune ought to be equalized in the interests of social justices. But earnings in the labour market are a different matter. Arguments about wages are not about social justice but about fairness in the determination of rewards for effort, skill and responsibilities at work, allowing for returns on investments in the acquisition of skills and the state of supply and demand in relation to varieties of skill. Very unequally endowed persons compete in a very imperfect labour market and the resulting structure of earnings is patently unfair. It is also socially unjust—but that is its nature and it must be corrected. If the elements of fortune were more equally distributed and the labour market were more perfect the distribution of earnings would be fairer. It might or might not also be more equal; but it is most unlikely to be socially just, since it would not have been constructed with rational regard to the variety of people's needs, deserts or choices and would need modification to bring it into line with these. Even a fair pay-structure would not enable us to dispense with the welfare state; though it is not hard to think of reasons connected with the aim of social justice why we should prefer a shallow to a steep gradient of inequality in the pay-structure, if we can get it without too great a sacrifice of economic efficiency— but this introduces the need for yet another investigation and yet another lecture.

Furthermore, the bundle of resources to the distribution of which we apply the principles of social justice represents opportunities not only for earnings but for enjoyment—enjoyment of the intrinsic satis- factions of skilled and responsible work of all kinds and of numerous cultural social advantages that are not directly relevant to work and earning power. Whatever, in the modern labour market, may be the relevance of educational opportunities to earning-power and earnings, this does not exhaust the significance of education to the promotion of social justice. It is a necessary condition for the making and realising of claims to *all* the necessities and amenities comprised in the notion of human well-being; it is inconceivable that public expenditure on education should be justified on any narrower basis than this.

I hope that you will not think that I have taken an unnecessarily long and circuitous route to reach a banal conclusion. It seems to me that Professor Jencks's book is forceful and persuasive, written as it is in an "easy" style, reassuringly backed by formidable but lucid foot- notes and appendices. Though many readers may feel uncomfortable in face of uncongenial, not to say provocative, propositions about educational problems and policies, they may not find it easy to seize on what seem to me to be profound defects in the argument.

However that may be, I want now to return briefly to Professor Meade's discussion of the inheritance of inequalities. I want to put before you the barest sketch of the workings of his model, taking into account the effects first, of the growing social practice of educating children in institutions outside the home and second, of the rise of the modern, publicly provided and financed educational system. I hope that this brief, bare and dry sketch will serve to remind us that the appropriate question is not whether schools can change people, but whether, other things being equal, the self-perpetuating momentum of the closed system of inherited inequalities can be checked by the injection of outside resources in the form of publicly provided education and training.

Professor Meade postulates an unreal world, in which marriages are permanent and monogamous, the labour market is competitive, the government non-interventionist and parents wholly responsible, directly or indirectly, for all the elements (including education and training) in the bundle of endowments they transmit to their children. In these deliberately simplified circumstances, the ultimate, self-perpetuating degree of inequality in the distribution of fortunes depends, as he explains, upon the interaction of three forces: (i) the tendency for like to marry like—for marriages to take place between partners in the same class position—for men with useful bundles of genes, property, education and social contact to marry women with similarly useful bundles of these elements of fortune; (ii) the tendency for random elements of chance to enter into the determination of people's genetic make-up and the events of their personal, social and economic lives and (iii) the production of feedbacks, positive and negative, in the system formed by the interacting elements of fortune. Thus, the greater the degree of assortative mating, the more numerous the random elements of chance and the more marked the positive feedbacks in the system, the greater will be the degree of ultimate inequality in the distribution of fortunes. These are the forces upon which state intervention must work if the objective is to equalize opportunities in the interests of social justice. We want to know what the scope and limitations of an attack on the system through an injection of public resources might be.

I have already explained that the element "education" in Professor Meade's model is defined in very broad terms to include practically all of the environmental influences which affect the development of an individual's knowledge, skill, character and motivation. I think it is illuminating to distinguish within this broad category between the diffuse and informal influences on character and motivation of upbringing, professional formation and social contacts from the knowledge and skills embodied in educational attainments and formal qualifications. For in a modern economy these latter are a necessary condition of occupational achievement and even Professor Meade's hypothetical, self-sufficient parents cannot provide them without having recourse to educational and training institutions outside the home. In its inclusive sense, the category education makes only for stability or positive feedback in the system of inequalities and never has the effect of diminishing a given degree of inequality in the distribution of fortunes. But the provision of education and training in institutions outside the home introduces new effects. The more that parents make use of such institutions the more widely children's educational endowments will vary according to their parents' incomes, wealth and size of family. Thus there will be more educational inequality in the system, and also more property inequality; for spending on their children's formal education and training will absorb resources that parents might otherwise save to accumulate property. But the implications for ultimate inequality in the distribution of fortunes will depend on the relative profitability of investment in education and property respectively. The evidence seems to show that in a modern economy the savings represented by the direct and indirect costs of an extended education could not be as profitably invested in other directions, so that increased spending on formal education and training would increase the ultimate inequality in the distribution of fortunes. At the same time and on the other hand, the self-perpetuating character of the system will be weakened by the greater scope for the random influences of chance. Parents may be well or badly informed about the institutions to which they decide to send their children; in any case, luck will affect the nature of personal encounters with teachers and friends in school and the outcome of these in successful or unsuccessful learning, helpful or unhelpful social contacts, fortunate or unfortunate choices of occupation and partners in marriage.

When formal education and training are provided at the taxpayer's expense, these effects are still further complicated. In the first place, the total amount of resources available for education will be increased. State expenditure will be financed from the proceeds of general taxation and many parents who would not or could not otherwise have provided formal education and training for their children will have them provided at public expense, free of cost to themselves except for children's earnings foregone. Many parents will not diminish the amount they spend on their children's education but will treat the free provision as a supplementary endowment; and many also will be stimulated to greater expenditure than they would otherwise have undertaken, especially on informal educational facilities such as books and travel and special tuition in subjects outside the school curriculum such as music and dancing or foreign languages.

The effect on educational inequality of this increase in total educational resources naturally depends on how they are distributed. Assuming general taxation to be progressive, if public funds are spent non-selectively on children in compulsory education in institutions of fairly uniform standard, the effect could hardly avoid being to some extent equalizing. If the distribution is selective according to children's needs—if, say, more is spent on handicapped or backward children, or on the children of poorer parents the equalizing effect will be stronger. But if the distribution is selective according to ability or "merit" or choice, then the effect is likely to be disequalizing notwithstanding the fact that many children among the able, the meritorious and the voluntary attenders in advanced courses will be drawn from the families of parents in humble circumstances. To obtain the maximum equalizing effect from a given amount of public educational resources, the distribution must be not only independent of, but negatively related to, the distribution of inherited inequalities of fortune, including genetic make-up. And the maximum effect will fall short of perfect equalization unless the amount of public educational resources is adequate to bring the fortune of the least well-endowed up to the size of that of the best endowed child. The self-perpetuating tendency of the ultimate distribution of fortunes will be checked to the extent that the publicly-provided institutions are socially and intellectually representative of the age group for which they provide, allowing the random influences of chance to discourage the assortative friendship and mating which perpetuate inherited inequalities of fortune. (If parents continue to provide private education, they increase the amount of educational resources available for general distribution, but they sustain the conservative influences of assortative friendships and mating on the ultimate degree of inequality).

These inferences from Professor Meade's model represent the bare bones of an educational policy intended to help equalize the distribution of inherited fortunes. His model solves no problems: for example, it does not help with the acute and forever absorbing political problem of reconciling the conflicting yet interdependent social objectives of justice, equality and economic efficiency; nor with the practical pedagogical problems of making the best use of available educational resources. What Professor Meade's model does is to show the systematic and complex nature of the social situation into which we must intervene if we want to diminish inequalities of inherited fortune, thus defining the theoretical scope and limitations of the contribution that educational policy can make to the achievement of this objective. He does not tell you whether or how education can help alleviate the social condition of poverty, nor whether you will do best with a given amount of resources to invest in nursery schools or junior colleges. But he does tell you that negative feedbacks can in principle be introduced with outside resources into the closed system of inherited inequalities of family background. It seems to me that in a climate of educational opinion which is as readily inclined to unwarranted pessimism as to unwarranted optimism, we need to be guided by just such meticulous analyses of the elements of the social situations to which educational policies are directed.

# References

Honoré, A. M. (1970). Social justice. In *Essays in Legal Philosophy*. Edited by R. S. Summers. Oxford: Blackwell and Mott. For a comprehensive and illuminating exposition of the principles of social justice.

Jencks, C. *et al.* (1972). *Inequality: A Reassessment of the Effect of Family and Schooling in America*. New York, London: Allen Lane.

Meade, J. E. (1973). The inheritance of inequalities. Some biological demographic, social and economic factors. *Proceedings of the British Academy*. **LIX.**

# Comprehensive Education: Internal Structure and Organization

## BRIAN SIMON

*School of Education, University of Leicester, Leicester, England*

Comprehensive education has been seen as a panacea for the nation's educational ills, or as the means by which the hard-won gains of centuries of educational endeavour may be brought to nought. Alternatively it is seen as an insurance against revolution (through social engineering), or as a subtle means of introducing socialism by the back door. The authors of the Black Papers of three or four years ago saw comprehensive education variously as a long stride towards totalitarianism on the one hand, and towards anarchy on the other. And so one might go on.

It is, of course, none of these. Although education is necessarily closely linked with politics, in that every educational change has political repercussions, comprehensive education is primarily an educational solution to educational problems. It represents the means of overcoming the increasingly sharp and evident contradictions—practical, theoretical and, I would add, ideological—which developed within the highly selective system inherited from the past—and between that system and economic, social and even political imperatives. Educational systems, particularly when they are designed to control the distribution of life chances (as the sociologists say) need some form of legitimization—and when the current legitimization no longer carries conviction, an unstable state sets in which requires regulation. This was the case with the 11+, with its reliance on particular theories derived from mental testing and the doctrine of limits—and the practical and organizational counterpart in rigid streaming both within individual primary schools and, through the triple-track system, the secondary system as a whole. In the circumstances the move to comprehensive education, which involved breaking down divisions and the development of a unified structure, was necessarily linked with the concept of opening up educational opportunity. Potentially—and I stress that word—it provides the means to educate the entire population; instead of building in, from the outset, methods of differentiation which militate against such an aim. In this sense the unification of secondary education marks (again, potentially) a new phase in educational and social practice.

My topic is the internal structure and organization of comprehensive schools—an aspect of vital significance and one of prime concern to practising educationists. This means jettisoning from the discussion many wider issues which are raised by the transition to comprehensive schooling—for instance how to develop a *genuinely* "comprehensive" system covering the country as a whole—or, even, specific and key urban areas such as London, Coventry, Manchester. I must leave aside the question of the independent or "public" schools, direct grant schools, voluntary aided schools or the school systems still largely under the control of religious bodies, and private schools of all kinds.

For complex historical reasons the move towards comprehensive education, which on the face of it might appear relatively simple and straightforward, runs up in this country against an array of vested interests or "traditions" closely woven into the social fabric which continue to provide a strong point for the defence of cherished advantages. But it must not be forgotten that these aspects relate closely to the realization of comprehensive education, and that in the long run they cannot be evaded.

That so much progress has been made in creating the new image of the single secondary school is in large part because teachers have, in this country, considerable freedom to determine the inner structure of schools. There are, of course, many constraints on this freedom—from local authority committees or officials, HMIs, governing bodies, parents associations, the national and local press. More specifically there are pressures from universities, or examining bodies, and the whole examination set-up. But if all these can exert an influence it remains the case that there is considerable scope for different solutions to problems of internal organization. These are likely to have profound educational and social implications—though, regrettably, little research evidence is yet available permitting anything very definite to be said on this score. But let us examine some of the options taken up and their rationale.

I shall confine myself to what might be called organization for teaching, to keep the subject within bounds. But this is to concentrate on what appears as a specific aspect in schools which have come to see their task in the wider framework of "socialization" and have evolved many methods to this end—especially in relation to arrangements for "pastoral care". These wider aspects must be borne in mind, since they are integral to the ethos of the common secondary school whose task is not merely to pass a selected few through to clerical occupations and universities but to provide for all who come "the chance to be men"—in the phrase used by one of the most notable of pre-war directors of education—H. G. Stead.

Two extreme forms of internal organization may be identified— related to the academic studies of the students and so to their cognitive developments: rigid or prismatic streaming on the one hand, and complete non-streaming on the other. Both embody—or are the practical manifestations of—opposite ideas about the nature of human learning and development.

The early comprehensive schools—those of twenty years ago or less—usually streamed their pupils on entry—though sometimes after a brief diagnostic period. This was then the current (and unquestioned) practice in both primary and secondary schools; legitimized, of course, by the theory that the child is born all that it might become—with which you in this society, in particular, will surely be familiar. If each child inherits a given, measurable "educable capacity", "intelligence" or verbal reasoning capacity as it was variously called, each must be provided with an education "appropriate" to that level. As Cyril Burt put it in a broadcast just at this time (1950):

"Obviously, in an ideal community, our aim should be to discover what ration of intelligence nature has given to each individual child at birth, then to provide him with the appropriate education, and finally to guide him into the career for which he seems to have been marked out."

This approach led directly to streaming which, in its classic form, meant grading children in a hierarchy of groups or classes on the basis of a prediction about their future intellectual development. Related to streaming was (and is) the system of setting, which is simply a more precise system of streaming by subject. These were then accepted as the only practical forms of internal school organization, both on grounds of humanity (since the child's nature was taken into account) and in terms of science.

This system is now often described as elitist—and accurately in the sense that the top streams were normally identified at, or soon after entry, and usually derived from the top (A) streams of the feeder primary schools. Elitism in this form continued in spite of the abolition of the 11+ in some areas and the bringing together of all the children in a given age group under one roof and one head and staff. In other words it was transposed basically unaltered to the comprehensive school—until experience dictated modifications.

In sharp contrast to this form of organization there are now some completely unstreamed comprehensive schools—at least to the age of sixteen. This approach is underpinned—whether altogether consciously or not—by a theoretical standpoint which, in contradistinction to that just outlined, stresses the power of teaching and education to bring about human change. Instead of being seen as an innate and fixed power, intelligence is regarded (to quote the well known definition from the Newsom Report) as "a variable that can be modified by social policy and educational approaches", or as "largely an acquired characteristic". In other words, as an amalgam of skills and abilities which can be learned in the process of education, itself seen as primarily concerned to *develop* human abilities, rather than simply register their existence or non-existence (Ministry of Education, 1963).

This case was expertly argued at this conference nearly ten years ago in 1965, by Douglas Pidgeon, then deputy director of the National Foundation of Educational Research. After rehearsing changing conceptions of "intelligence" he drew the conclusion that "the grouping of children" in comprehensive schools "in terms of their apparent abilities must be eschewed"—groups should be heterogeneous in character (Pidgeon, 1966). It is to this conclusion that a growing number of teachers in such schools have come.

If it is held that the student's activity in its social setting is an important determinant of development, it follows that streaming must be rejected since this itself provides an environment which necessarily sets limits to development. Streaming, in other words, is a self-fulfilling prophecy—empirical evidence in support of this was made available by, among others, J. W. B. Douglas up to ten years ago (Douglas, 1964).

It might be said that the non-streamed situation is *the best means known to us now* of providing an educational environment most conducive to the development of *all* the pupils in a school. Leaving aside the social benefits, any other form of grouping is likely to lead to lowered expectations on the part of the teachers for some of the students, to lower aspirations on the part of these students, and hence to a lower level of development by these than might otherwise have been achieved. I stress the phrase "known to us now" as there is some evidence that forms of grouping which retain the essential features of non-streaming but which are based on one or other specific criterion (for instance "teachability") may conceivably provide more·effectively for develop-

## TABLE I

### First-year grouping by type of school in Britain, 1968, and 1971 sample survey (schools 11+ and 12+-intake only)

| Method of grouping | Percentage of schools (numbers in brackets) | | | | | Total number of schools | Per-centage 1968 | 1971 Sample survey Percentage of schools |
| --- | --- | --- | --- | --- | --- | --- | --- | --- |
| | 11/12–18(I) | 11/12–18(II) | 11/12–16 | 11/12–13 | 11/12–14/15 | | | |
| 1. In streams | 17·5 | 13 | 20·5 | 34 | 23 | 130 | 19·5 | 4·5 |
| 2. In broad ability bands | 34·5 | 32 | 27 | 21 | 26 | 210 | 31 | 45 |
| 3. In sets | 4 | 16 | 8 | 7 | 20 | 36 | 5·5 | 3·5 |
| 4. Combination of streams and sets | 12 | 16 | 18 | 14 | 17 | 96 | 14·5 | 5·5 |
| 5. Mixed ability (I) (no more than two subjects setted) | 5 | 10 | 8 | 14 | 1 | 42 | 6 | 10 |
| 6. Mixed ability (2) (remedial pupils separated) | 14 | 13 | 9·5 | 10 | 7 | 80 | 12 | 18 |
| 7. Mixed ability (3) (for all subjects and pupils) | 5 | 6 | 2 | | 6 | 29 | 4 | 6·5 |
| 8. Other method | 7 | 10 | 6 | | 6 | 43 | 6·5 | 7 |
| Unknown | 1 | | 1 | | 4 | 7 | 1 | |
| Total number of schools | 100(389) | 100(31) | 100(154) | 100(29) | 100(70) | 673 | 100 | 100(111) |

Source: Benn and Simon (1972), p. 219.

ment. The whole question of the "best" form of grouping (in relation to cognitive development) within the classroom is a highly complex one which has been neglected and requires research—and I don't mean only the obsolete comparison of streaming and non-streaming.

We have, then, two dichotomous forms, or systems, of internal school organization each powered, as it were, by opposite ideas as to the nature of the child and learning, yet both existing concurrently. But of course, generally speaking, things are not so clear cut. There is much confusion on the theoretical side—and this is understandable since psychologists are themselves divided into opposing camps or take up what appear to the layman as irreconcilable positions—while, in addition, teachers are subject to practical pressures and a variety of constraints. While it would be hard now to find a single 11–18 comprehensive school organized throughout on the elitist model, there are as yet no more than a handful of schools which mirror the unstreamed model outlined. But Table I, which embodies the results of two surveys of the internal organization of comprehensive schools in Britain in 1968 and 1971 indicates a clear and even dramatic swing towards the latter model at least in the earlier years of secondary schooling. The percentage of 11+ and 12+ comprehensive schools which allocated children to streams in their first year declined over these three years from 19·5 to 4·5 while those allotting children to unstreamed "mixed ability" classes of one kind or another (adding together categories 5, 6, 7) rose from 22% to 34·5%. This indicates a practical striving towards the latter model. In short, schools are now in a state of transition; structures of internal organization are being developed which, if showing a certain trend, in fact embody (as the table shows) every kind of compromise.

Some of the patterns indicated are worth attention.

1. Table I shows that the most popular form of inner school organization involves "banding" (Category 2)—the division of pupils into 2, 3 or 4 broad "ability" bands for teaching and learning—within each band pupils may either be setted or placed in homogeneous groups. While this represents a rejection of prismatic streaming, it preserves a sharp distinction between broad groups of pupils and represents, therefore, a compromise situation.

2. Again it is a common experience in comprehensive schools to find that the mathematics and modern languages departments are the most reluctant to relinquish streaming or setting; category 5 reflects this situation—10% of schools in the 1971 survey, though otherwise unstreamed, retain setting in one or two

subjects—which is justified on the grounds of the essentially sequential nature of these disciplines.

3. Categories 6 and 7 bring out another area of controversy—how to provide best for the backward or "slow learning" children, those with severe learning difficulties (other than ESN) variously estimated as comprising between 10 and 15 per cent of the age group.

In most schools which use streaming, setting or banding, these are normally segregated for teaching purposes. As the table shows (Category 6) quite a high proportion—about half—of schools otherwise (unstreamed also segregate these in special classes of their own, even though the rest of the school is not streamed in the first year. A relatively small proportion of schools otherwise unstreamed bring these in with the rest of the pupils (Category 8 which comprises about one fifth of *unstreamed* schools in 1968, rising to one quarter in 1971). Yet this latter solution appears to have widespread support among those who teach these children. This system which ensures that these pupils spend most of their time with normal pupils, involves withdrawal from normal classes for special assistance by a qualified teacher, and/or assistance in the normal classroom situation by a remedial teacher who comes in for that purpose.

Many other examples of allocation, or divisive, procedures might be given. For instance, the provision of special, non-examination courses for what used to be known as "Newsom" pupils—those who, it was predicted, would leave at the earliest opportunity and who in any case were alienated from normal school work. More recently courses for those newly staying on until sixteen, the so-called ROSLA pupils, have taken the same form. Then there is the powerful influence of the General Certificate of Education and CSE—the Certificate of Secondary Education. Unless deliberate steps are consciously taken to overcome these there is imposed a threefold division in the middle school—the GCE band, the CSE and the non-examination or "Newsom/ROSLA" group. In this sense "broad banding" from eleven corresponds to the realities of the examination system, designed well before comprehensive education was on the order of the day— and now a chief target for criticism, or a key point to be defended, depending on the point of view.

It can, of course, be argued that the school must build in differentiating systems of this kind, since its primary social function is that of a distributor of life chances, and this must be related to the occupational structure of society, which still demands a large pool of unskilled and therefore untutored labour, a lesser pool destined for skilled labour and a still smaller group qualified to fill the clerical, minor professional and fully professional or managerial areas. But this is not the form in which the issue presents itself to teachers in developing comprehensive schools. These are increasingly led, in spite of all the difficulties, which are legion, to seek the best means of educating *all* their pupils without distinction. The survival of ideas and practices which promote divisions within the school is in part due to the very long drawn out transition to comprehensive education; to obstacles consistently faced from its very inception, including justification of comprehensive education in terms of such tripartite criteria as successes in GCE equivalent to those of selective grammar schools—while continuing uncertainties about future developments in material terms and in terms of planning have had their effect. I have suggested that, by a process of evolution, comprehensive schools have moved, or are moving, from an overtly selective form of internal organization to more flexible approaches which recognize the undesirability of docketing children and thereby confining, or streamlining, their development from an early age. What we are experiencing now is a *process* of change—of transition from what might be called the pre-war model (in conceptual terms) to a model reflecting new knowledge and experience as to learning and teaching and the organizational forms required to maximize these. I emphasize the *transitional* nature of the present phase deliberately, because it is necessary to guard against a possible danger—that sociologists may confuse (or obfuscate) matters by setting an undue stamp on certain features of the present situation.

An attempt has been made by a sympathetic analyst of comprehensive education to describe the present situation in terms of meritocratic or egalitarian objectives identifying characteristic organizational forms accordingly. While the meritocratic school, writes Dennis Marsden, "seeks primarily to maximize the academic attainments of children from all social backgrounds", the "egalitarian" school "also lays stress on broader educational aims and is intended to become a solvent for inequalities and social tensions in society".

The meritocratic school is characterized (in its internal organization) by "streamed, competitive, formal, academic class teaching" with "specialist" teachers for the "high flyers" while the egalitarian school uses "non-streamed, cooperative, 'progressive' and flexible (e.g. team) teaching and discriminates positively towards the less able". The former provides a varied curriculum with "individual time-tables of specialisms" and promotes the "sorting" of children, counselling and "the discovery of individual skill", while the egalitarian promotes a common curriculum (albeit "with individualized learning") and delays specialization. The meritocratic school measures success by "academic attainment, O- and A-levels, large sixth forms, large university entrance and high quality in maths and science "while the egalitarian emphasizes" general education, out of school activities, mixing across social classes, good relations with the surrounding community, and high quality in 'non-examinable' subjects like art, music and drama" (Marsden, 1969).

I do not think that matters are as simple as this, and categorization of this kind may well create a conceptual dichotomy which bears little relation to the more complex actuality, so reducing rather than aiding our ability to define fruitful ways ahead out of the present transitional stage. In this connection the findings of another analysis, by a comprehensive school headmaster are of interest. Dr Thompson examined in a very normal urban all-through comprehensive school (a neighbourhood school in Coventry) a move from rigid streaming to complete non-streaming over a period of several years and found that the move to a so-called "egalitarian" internal structure was accompanied by highly significant improvements in terms of the two indicators used—examination results in GCE O-level and rates of staying on. These are given in Tables II and III. Table II show the percentage staying on for the full five years (before the raising of the leaving age)—first, when entrants had been streamed in 1961 into ten classes, and second when in 1965 entrants were placed in unstreamed classes in which they remained for two years. While of the 1961 entrants the percentage staying on varies from 86 to 0 (diminishing hierarchically), the 1965 entrants' staying on rate varied across all classes only between 72% and 48%—while the average staying on rate increased from 38% to 64%.

A similar, but perhaps more striking, pattern for GCE O-level results is shown in Table III which gives the percentage of first year forms eventually gaining one or more GCE O-level passes. Here again the strictly hierarchical pattern of the streamed 1961 entrants contrasts strikingly with the pattern achieved by non-streaming where, with possibly a couple of exceptions (IE and IS) every class achieved roughly similar results, while the move to complete non-streaming was accompanied by a doubling of the average percentage gaining one or more O-level passes.

Incidentally, in view of the main objection to comprehensive education, it is worth noting that Dr Thompson's evidence indicates that those who benefited *most* from the abandonment of streaming were those usually classified as "high flyers" (Thompson, 1972).

## TABLE II
### The Woodlands School, Coventry

Percentage of first year forms completing the five year course

| | 1A | 1B | 1C | 1D | 1E | 1F | 1G | 1H | 1S | 1T | Average |
|---|---|---|---|---|---|---|---|---|---|---|---|
| 1961 % | 86 | 60 | 55 | 57 | 30 | 21 | 19 | 11 | 0 | 0 | 38% |
| | 1T | 1H | 1E | 1W | 1O | 1D | 1L | 1A | 1N | 1S | Average |
| 1965 % | 71 | 65 | 70 | 72 | 56 | 57 | 64 | 71 | 48 | 70 | 64% |

Source: *FORUM* (Thompson, 1972).

## TABLE III
### The Woodlands School, Coventry

Percentage of first year forms eventually gaining one or more 'O' level passes

| | 1A | 1B | 1C | 1D | 1E | 1F | 1G | 1H | 1S | 1T | Average |
|---|---|---|---|---|---|---|---|---|---|---|---|
| 1961 entry % | 71 | 50 | 41 | 32 | 7 | 3 | 0 | 4 | 0 | 0 | 23·4 |
| | 1T | 1H | 1E | 1W | 1O | 1D | 1L | 1A | 1N | 1S | Average |
| 1965 entry % | 57 | 50 | 52 | 48 | 33 | 43 | 56 | 55 | 33 | 44 | 47·2 |

Source: *FORUM* (Thompson, 1972).

In other words this investigator found that an "egalitarian" form of internal organization "operated by a staff that believed in and is dedicated to the idea of non-streaming" achieved what Marsden, as a sociologist, describes as élitist objectives more effectively than the traditional meritocratic form of organization. This research—the first and only example of its kind so far as I am aware—seems to underline that the introduction of new classificatory dichotomies may be misconceived and misleading.

Teachers, as I have suggested earlier, necessarily approach matters at a different level from researchers and a whole variety of considerations may influence the way changes are made and how they are introduced—the size, amenities and staffing of schools, the areas they serve, besides lesser internal factors. In 1968, in the enquiry conducted by Caroline Benn and myself and published in *Half Way There* (1972), it was found that 80% of comprehensive schools in England and Wales ran a common course for all pupils for the first year (eleven to twelve years of age) but approximately half of these (48%) ran such a course for three years. Most of these organized the course at different levels (as is indicated in Table I) but there were then already forty-two comprehensive schools that arranged for this on a .non-streamed basis for the full three years. (These figures, it should be noted, are now six years out of date.)

Here it is evident that curricular considerations are a major aspect in the decision to obviate streaming. The first three years of secondary school life, from eleven to fourteen, involves the realization of basically common objectives for all pupils which can be embodied in a common curriculum (or, better, common educational experiences) which, in turn, can well be taught without selective organization of classes. But non-streaming is only a negative criterion, indicating the rejection of a particular and longstanding form of grouping whose negative features are evident; the essential decision to be taken is what alternative method is to be adopted.

Once streaming (ABC) by ability, or present achievement level, is set aside teachers tend to talk of "mixed ability" classes for want of a better term. This merely implies that the aim of setting up "homogeneous" classes in terms of attainment and present apparent potential has been abandoned rather than establishing any clear criterion. What it does do, however, is open up a wide variety of options relating to allocation to classes or teaching units several of which are in fact taken up—though I know of little or no research bearing on the matter. Here are some examples:

1. random sampling;
2. balanced "mixed ability", i.e. each class having the same proportion of different ability bands as measured by mental testing;
3. friendship grouping;
4. neighbourhood grouping, keeping children from the same districts together; or alternatively,
5. neighbourhood scattering grouping (the opposite principle);
6. social class, or parental occupation, grouping, so as to ensure that each class has an equivalent "social mix";
7. personality grouping (suggested recently by Eysenck);
8. linked with this, grouping for "teachability", i.e. matching specific teachers and pupils as proposed by the American educationist, Thelen;
9. balanced sex grouping, or presumably, the opposite.

There will always be much discussion and consideration in addition about how to deal with the handicapped, the backward in a particular basic subject, the slow learner, the "high flyer" or the type of child who is a problem in any form of organization including traditional streaming.

Once embarked on this kind of basic discussion and decision making about internal organization, comprehensive schools cannot avoid important theoretical issues. On the way they are resolved depends the formulation of objectives for the school as a whole, not merely the lower school; and these will provide the framework for working out the curriculum in all its aspects and the pedagogical means whereby objectives can be achieved—whether relating to systems of grouping, methods of promoting learning, or systems of teaching. Circumstances compel every comprehensive school to resolve such issues in one way or another, the decisions taken being crystallized in the time-table which itself reflects the form of inner school organization. This is in sharp contrast to the previous position when the divided structure of the school system reflected a clear functional division between the grammar school—which theoretically purveyed academic education to an elite, and the modern school, intended to purvey a banausic—or what is variously described as a folk/pluralist/relativist (depending on your authority) culture to 80% of the children, the excluded masses. In this sense it is only with the introduction of the comprehensive school that the crucial *educational* issues come to the fore, not merely in terms of endeavouring to provide *all* children with the level of education necessary to function effectively in a modern industrialized society— with many internal problems of its own—in the latter half of the twentieth century; but also in terms of what *kind* of education this should be.

The provision of a common curriculum—or common educational experiences—is, I suggest, a more logical objective for the comprehensive school than the harmonization of different social classes or other aspects of social engineering which have been advanced. This is, of course, a key question for the comprehensive school since objectives in terms of learning must determine organization. A common curriculum makes possible a unified form of organization.

It is both exhilarating and exacting for teachers in these schools to find how far the smallest step in reconstructing internal organization may take them. While the lower school may present relatively few problems in this respect, more difficult issues arise in relation to the fourteen to sixteen age group.

The three tier system imposed on schools by the examination system —framed before comprehensive reorganization—has already been referred to. GCE was designed for the selective grammar schools, CSE for the next 40% of the so-called "ability range" then located in modern schools—when the demand of these schools for an examination, initially ruled out, could no longer be withstood. Given this structure, it is hard to allow for unforeseen development on the part of individual children, since preparation for an examination involves following an allotted path.

Hence, as a result of developments in the internal organization of comprehensive schools, comes the call for single examination at sixteen—even, and with influential support, for the abolition of any external examination at sixteen at all. Those arguing for a single examination—which, as I understand it, has the support of the Schools Council—propose using modern procedures developed by CSE examiners such as assessment of course work, teacher control and so on. The case for a single examination has been enhanced by the raising of the leaving age to sixteen. Though apparently still in the balance, this reform would simplify the problem of internal organization very greatly, facilitate the realization of educational objectives and so diminish divisions or inequalities within the schools. Meanwhile some schools are gaining experience in unifying the curriculum of the middle years which will certainly be of value in the future. They are able to do this only by careful planning and using such possibilities as exist within the present structure. This involves bringing CSE and GCE courses into relation with each other by special arrangements with specific examining boards. Schools like Hedley Wood School in Brentwood and Countesthorpe College in Leicestershire have found it possible so to unify internal organization over the fourteen to sixteen age range. By this means *all* students—as such schools prefer to call their pupils—are enabled to follow the common course (allowing for considerable individual choice and diversity) leading at present equally to examinations at different levels—or, indeed, by-passing the examination altogether.

It is one of the basic fallacies of educational discussion, if by no means the only one, that experiment properly only takes place outside the publicly provided school system. A contingent one is that to introduce a common secondary school is to impose drab uniformity or reduce matters to the lowest common denominator. Possibly, as I have suggested, the variety in forms of organization both of school systems as a whole and of internal structures is now almost too great. Certainly much more could be done to pool experience and make a more planned attack on the key questions—although as things have been, and still are, it is perhaps as well that the Department of Education and Science has shown so little interest in comprehensive developments and that it has lain with the schools and teachers to take the initiative.

## References

Benn, C. and Simon, B. (1972). *Half Way There*. Harmondsworth, Middlesex: Penguin Books.
Burt, C. (1950). *The Listener*, 16 March.
Douglas, J. W. B. (1964). *The Home and the School*. London: MacGibbon and Kee.
Marsden, D. (1969). *Comprehensive Education*, No. 13 Autumn.
Ministry of Education (1963). *Half our Future* (The "Newsom Report"). Report of the Central Advisory Council for Education. London: HMSO.
Pidgeon, D. (1966). Intelligence testing and comprehensive education. In *Genetic and Environmental Factors in Human Ability*. Edited by J. E. Meade and A. S. Parkes. Edinburgh: Oliver and Boyd.
Thompson, D. (1972). *Forum* **16,** 2.

# Examinations in Education

## DESMOND L. NUTTALL

*Schools Council, London, England*

I must at the outset make it clear that I am going to confine most of my discussion to public examinations taken by secondary-school children, namely the Certificate of Secondary Education (CSE) and the Ordinary level of the General Certificate of Education (GCE), which are usually taken at the age of sixteen, and the Advanced level of the GCE, normally taken at eighteen. In British education, there is of course a multiplicity of other examinations, from the 11+ at one end of the spectrum to university finals and professional examinations at the other, but my experience only qualifies me to talk with any real knowledge about CSE and GCE. More importantly, the Schools Council has responsibilities for only these public examinations; specifically these responsibilities fall under two headings:

1. the co-ordination of secondary-school examinations in England and Wales;
2. the tendering of advice to the Secretary of State for Education and Science on matters of examinations policy.

Secondary-school examinations have never been as much in demand as they are today. In Summer 1972 (the last year for which official figures are available) no less than 844,847 individuals were candidates for GCE O- and A-level and for CSE—a small proportion of these were adults taking evening classes or studying by correspondence, but it would be safe to say that 750,000 of this group were between the ages of fifteen and nineteen. Between them, these students entered for 1·35 million CSE subject examinations, 2·30 million GCE O-level subject examinations and 470,000 GCE A-level subject examinations (Department of Education and Science, 1974). These figures predate the effect of the raising of the school-leaving age, and all the signs are that the numbers of candidates and subject entries in Summer 1974 will be substantially larger, particularly in the case of the CSE.

67

Why this massive volume of examining, that might almost be termed an industry? Why are schools, teachers, parents and pupils prepared to see virtually the whole of every summer term devoted to examinations, which disrupt the normal activities of the school? To attempt to answer these questions, I would like first to take a brief look at the history of examinations. Historians of examinations (e.g. Morris, 1961) invariably trace their origins to the Chinese Empire in the days of the first millenium BC. Competition for the Imperial Service was intense and nepotism was rife; in an attempt to stamp out nepotism and bribery, a system of practical examinations was instituted, involving horse-riding, archery and other such skills. Over the years, the system evolved placing more emphasis on academic skills, through the medium of written papers, and less on practical skills. The final result was, then, a system of highly competitive examinations not unlike the current scholarship examinations set by colleges at Cambridge and Oxford. There then is a Dark Age for examinations, and apart from the *viva voce* examinations at degree level, examinations only began to be instituted in this country in the early nineteenth century. It is interesting to note that the major reason for their introduction was identical to that which led the Chinese to establish them, namely to eliminate nepotism and other unfair practices. Later in the nineteenth century, the old-established universities, worried about selection and academic standards, instituted their own mechanisms for examining schools and school-children. The first of these examination boards was the Oxford Delegacy of Local Examinations which was established in 1858, but other universities were not slow to follow suit. Co-ordination among these boards only came, however, after the great upheavals, both in education and in society, in the early twentieth century. In 1918, the boards were asked to bring in a uniform system known as the School Certificate and Higher School Certificate. The School Certificate examination system remained virtually unchanged, until following the Norwood Report (Board of Education, 1943) and the Butler 1944 Education Act, the School Certificate was replaced by the General Certificate of Education in which the first examinations were set in 1951. Apart from the fact that the GCE was to be a single-subject examination in contrast to the grouping of subjects in the School Certificate, the changes were relatively small and so this system persists to this day. Of course, relatively minor changes to grading schemes have been made over the years and major changes have taken place in the techniques of examining and assessing pupils, but the essential philosophy of the system remains, in my view, virtually unaltered. The GCE examination, like the School Certificate before it, was primarily designed to be an examination in academic subjects aimed at pupils in grammar and public schools, in other words, the "elite" 20 to 30% of children in the age group. It was not long before many other schools were entering candidates, in many cases inappropriately, for the GCE, and other examination bodies (such as the Royal Society of Arts and the London Chamber of Commerce) were setting examinations for the secondary-modern child. Local examinations also began to proliferate, and to bring order into increasing chaos, the Minister of Education set up a committee, under the chairmanship of Beloe, to see if the system could be rationalized. The Beloe Report (Ministry of Education, 1960) recommended the establishment of the Certificate of Secondary Education. The essential features of the CSE system were:

1. that it was designed for pupils between the 40th and 80th percentiles of ability; i.e. essentially for schoolchildren who would not be continuing in full-time education, and
2. that it was to be an examination controlled by school-teachers, and hence organized on a regional basis.

The first CSE examinations were set in 1965 (the year after the Schools Council was established to take over the responsibilities, in relation to public examinations, of the Secondary Schools Examinations Council) and since 1965, the CSE has expanded dramatically; in the case of some boards, the number of subject entries in Summer 1974 show increases of more than 70% over the number in 1973. In the last decade, the expansion has been of the order of some 400 per cent. If CSE and GCE O-level are considered together, it is almost certainly true to say that 80% of sixteen-year-olds in England and Wales took one or more public examinations in Summer 1974.

This brief historical review has illustrated some of the main reasons why the proponents of public examinations believe that these examinations are an essential feature of the educational system. I now wish to consider the reasons in more detail before I turn to look briefly at some of the possible alternatives to public examinations.

The prime function of public examinations is undoubtedly to assess the attainment of an individual at the end of a course of study. Chief Examiners and Chief Moderators direct virtually all their attention to ensuring that the examination is a fair and comprehensive test of what has been taught and learned, and that the results it yields are as precise and reliable as possible. Linked with this function is that of the maintenance of educational standards; by having a nationally-validated system of public examinations, justice can be seen to be done and society may judge for itself one very important aspect of the efficiency of the educational system. Also linked to these functions is the licensing function of examinations. Most professional qualifications serve this function: many of those who defend external examinations take great delight in asking whether you would be prepared to subject yourself to the surgeon's knife if you were not certain that his peers and teachers had judged him competent to wield it. The sort of examinations that I am discussing do not really have this licensing function to any great degree, but perhaps employers, further and higher education look for passes in English language and mathematics, in particular, as indicators of general competence.

These three interlinked functions—the assessment of attainment, the maintenance of standards, and licensing—raise what, to many, is the crucial issue in any discussion of public examinations, namely central control of the curriculum. To my mind, this is a political issue and a professional issue, a matter for teachers and politicians to debate, and I do not therefore propose to discuss it at length. Nevertheless one must accept that much of the discussion and debate that centres around public examinations in the teaching profession, and in the Schools Council itself, is primarily concerned with the issue of who should be responsible for what is taught in schools. This issue is not, of course, unique to this country, but my reading of the political entrails is that this issue is going to emerge further from the shadows in the next few years; indeed, I believe one has only to look across the Atlantic to see the twin spectres of "educational accountability" and "teacher-proof curriculum packages" to realise the directions in which the debate might move.

A further function of examinations, clearly seen from the days of the Chinese Empire, is as instruments of selection. I am neither a politician nor a sociologist and I therefore trust that I am not being naive in suggesting that some form of selection will always be with us. We may see the day when we have universal comprehensive secondary education, and perhaps we might see the day when we have a comprehensive system of further and higher education, but I cannot foresee the day when all jobs and professions are going to be equally attractive and the forces of supply and demand will be in balance. While we still have selection in secondary and tertiary education, we are obliged to consider whether examinations are either a desirable or necessary part of the selection process. Recent research at the National Foundation for Educational Research has shown that A-levels are, by and large, rather poor predictors of success at university, where success is measured in terms of the class of one's final degree (NFER, 1973). The same research showed that a Test of Academic Aptitude, modelled on the American Scholastic Aptitude Test, was, generally speaking, a rather worse predictor of university success than A-levels and, indeed, added virtually nothing to the efficiency of prediction of A-level in multiple regression analyses. Other educational researchers are investigating the potential of non-cognitive measures as predictors; there is some evidence that such measures, for example of achievement motivation and study habits as well as of dimensions of personality, can enhance the predictive efficiency of A-levels, but on their own do not match the predictive efficiency of A-levels (e.g. Entwistle, 1974). No selector is, of course, ever likely to use A-levels or psychometric measures (or both) without recourse to other evidence obtained from interviews and references; even so, examination results currently play a key role both as screening devices and as selection devices.

Before passing on to look at the way in which employers use examination results, I would like to refer to the perennial problem that faces the psychometrician, the criterion problem. In the research that I have been discussing, the criterion of success was the class of one's final degree. This has the merit of being quantifiable—though there are scaling problems—but does it really describe comprehensively what success at university comprises? Even if it is a valid measure of success, which Einstein and Darwin would have doubted (Hudson, 1964), is it reliable and comparable from university to university? Could we devise a measure of success that was more valid, more reliable and more comparable? I doubt it. If I am right, then it might be fair to say that the relative lack of predictive efficiency of A-levels lies partly on the side of the criterion measure of success. In practice, the blame (if such it may be described) probably lies equally on both sides of the walls of the ivory towers of our universities. Two further points need to be made: first, A-levels are designed primarily as measures of attainment, not as measures of future potential, and, secondly, there is an important technical factor which will always make a high level of predictive efficiency difficult to obtain; that is, the marked homogeneity of the population of university applicants.

No discussion of the criterion problem can be complete without a mention of the phenomenon described by Professors Wall and Simon earlier today. This is the phenomenon of the self-fulfilling prophecy (Pidgeon, 1970), described more graphically by Rosenthal and Jacobson (1968) as "Pygmalion in the classroom". Such writers tell us, in effect, that the predictive efficiency of examinations such as the 11+ is as good as it proved to be (e.g. Yates and Pidgeon, 1957) because of the effect that the knowledge of· results had on the attitudes and behaviour of the pupils, their teachers and their parents. It would be interesting to know if such writers would feel that part of the predictive efficiency of A-levels is due to this same effect. If they feel so and are correct in their feeling, the burden of the Admissions Tutor can be somewhat lifted—from now on, all he really needs is a pin!

Employers, particularly of young school-leavers, appear to be ambivalent in their attitudes towards examinations. No large-scale survey of their selection policies has been carried out and I agree with Jennings (1974) that such a survey is long overdue. National bodies of employers and many professions have for years stipulated minimum requirements in terms of performance in public examinations and these minimum requirements are becoming stiffer and stiffer; ten years ago, a professional body might have demanded five passes at GCE O-level: today, they would be more likely to demand two passes at A-level and a further three at O-level. To what extent they discriminate among those applicants who have achieved the minimum requirements on the basis of their examination results is not clear, and practices obviously vary. Nevertheless, it is quite apparent that employers set considerable store by the results of public examinations and a leader writer in the *Guardian* on 17 January 1974 had this to say on the subject:

> "When some teachers say that public examinations can be bad indicators of a student's ultimate ability they are probably right. But even if O- and A-levels and CSEs do not necessarily reveal much about an individual's real ability it does not follow that they are worthless. Even if some teachers dismiss them as false prophets of ability, employers do not. Rightly or wrongly a CSE, an O-level, or an A-level is a passport. Employers and universities recognize them as such. A school-leaver without one has left school at a disadvantage in a world which has begun to ask shoe-shop assistants for O-levels in English and Mathematics.

> "There are, of course, still plenty of jobs which do not demand O-levels. But most of them are deadends. Some of them are jobs which will soon be done by a machine that is about to be invented. Moreover the people in the deadend jobs soon notice where they are heading and resent it. A student who for one reason or another has been inadequate at school feels inadequate again—not necessarily to the extent of throwing bricks through windows but certainly to the extent of feeling that his school has let him down. And perhaps it has."

The impact of public examinations on the individual pupil and on the teacher must then be of central concern. It is perhaps a condemnation of myself and other research workers in the field of public examinations that I can do no better than to quote from the 1911 Report of the

Consultative Committee on Examinations in Secondary Schools, but I have the comfort of knowing that this passage has also been quoted by Wiseman (1961), who called it a "forgotten classic", and in the Beloe Report (Ministry of Education, 1960). The passage reads as follows:

"It will be convenient if we summarize what we believe to be the more important effects of examinations (1) on the pupil, (2) on the teacher:

1. The good effects of examinations on the pupil are
   a. that they make him work up to time by requiring him to reach a stated degree of knowledge by a fixed date;
   b. that they incite him to get his knowledge into reproducible form and to lessen the risk of vagueness;
   c. That they make him work at parts of a study which, though important, may be uninteresting or repugnant to him personally;
   d. that they train the power of getting up a subject for a definite purpose, even though it may not appear necessary to remember it afterwards—a training which is useful for parts of the professional duty of the lawyer, the administrator, the journalist, and the man of business, and secretary;
   e. that in some cases they encourage a certain steadiness of work over a long period of time; and
   f. that they enable the pupil to measure his real attainment:
      (i) by the standard required by outside examiners,
      (ii) by comparison with the attainment of his fellow-pupils, and
      (iii) by comparison with the attainments of his contemporaries in other schools.
   On the other hand, examinations may have a bad effect upon the pupil's mind
   a. by setting a premium on the power of merely reproducing other people's ideas and other people's methods of presentment, thus diverting energy from the creative process;
   b. by rewarding evanescent forms of knowledge;
   c. by favouring a somewhat passive type of mind;
   d. by giving an unfair advantage to those who, in answering questions on paper, can cleverly make the best use of, perhaps, slender attainments;
   e. by inducing the pupil, in his preparation for an examination, to aim rather at absorbing information imparted to him by the teacher than at forming an independent judgement upon the subjects in which he received instruction; and
   f. by stimulating the competitive (and, at its worst, a mercenary) spirit in the acquisition of knowledge.
2. The good effects of well-conducted examinations upon the teacher are
   a. that they induce him to treat his subject thoroughly;
   b. that they make him so arrange his lessons as to cover with intellectual

thoroughness a prescribed course of study within appointed limits
of time;

c. that they impel him to pay attention not only to his best pupils, but
also to the backward and the slower amongst those who are being
prepared for the examination; and

d. that they make him acquainted with the standard which other
teachers and their pupils are able to reach in the same subject in
other places of education.

On the other hand, the effects of examination on the teacher are bad:

a. in so far as they constrain him to watch the examiner's foibles and
to note his idiosyncrasies (or the tradition of the examination) in
order that he may arm his pupils with the kind of knowledge
required for dealing successfully with the questions that will
probably be put to them;

b. in so far as they limit the freedom of the teacher in choosing the way
in which he shall treat his subject;

c. in so far as they encourage him to take upon himself work which
had better be left to the largely unaided efforts of his pupils,
causing him to impart information to them in too digested a form or
to select for them groups of facts or aspects of the subject which
each pupil should properly be left to collect or envisage for himself;

d. in so far as they predispose the teacher to overvalue among his
pupils that type of mental development which secures success in
examinations;

e. in so far as they make it the teacher's interest to excel in the purely
examinable side of his professional work and divert his attention
from those parts of education which cannot be tested by the process
of examination."

I have attempted to show that examinations serve a useful function
in education and society, and are likely to do so for some time to come.
If public examinations were to be abolished, it is difficult to see what
would take their place. The danger is that each employer, professional
body, institute of higher and further education would establish their
own selection procedures. Young people would perhaps go from
employer to employer, taking battery after battery of aptitude and
attainment tests—in many cases, probably the same battery of tests—
and the end result might well be anarchical. Interestingly enough, it
was the existence of a very similar kind of anarchy that led to the
establishment of the CSE, within which control of the syllabuses and
assessment techniques rested, and still rests, with the teaching profession.

Is there a middle course to steer between the elaborate machinery
of a public examination system and no public examinations at all? I

believe there is. I have been careful not to define too closely what is meant by the term "public examination". Most of us remember the system as it was some years ago when a public examination tended to mean two three-hour written papers often taken on the same day at the height of summer. The public examinations of today are often very different, particularly in the CSE. Internal assessment by the candidate's own teacher of oral work, project work and general coursework very often counts for up to 50% of the candidate's mark. No longer is it is a case of teacher and pupil trying to defeat the "outsiders", the external examiners. Assessment becomes part and parcel of the teaching process. This internal assessment need not necessarily be on work derived from a syllabus laid down by an examination board. The syllabus may be devised by the teacher in part or in whole. In the latter case, an internal syllabus examined by internal assessment, an option available in both GCE and CSE, where it is known as Mode 3, we reach a position where, in my view, we have nearly all the advantages of examinations as expounded in the 1911 Report and few of the disadvantages. But such a system requires a validating stage, the process of moderation, so that these internal examinations can yield results which are nationally valid. The Schools Council is currently conducting an evaluation of moderation techniques; all I can say at the present time is that, to be successful, such techniques demand money and, above all, the time of experienced teachers.

Other countries are moving towards much more internal assessment which is then externally moderated to yield nationwide, or at least regional, comparability of standards. Two examples are New Zealand and some Australian states. This system permits great flexibility in the curriculum from school to school. This same freedom is not apparent in countries such as France and Germany which appear on the surface to have no examination at the age when compulsory schooling ends; and the often-quoted example of Sweden (Henrysson, 1964), where moderation is done by way of a nationally-set common core reference test (rather than by visiting moderators) and where the test consequently tends to define a national curriculum, is unlikely to be of much help to us in England.

Externally-moderated internal assessment is then an option which is already open to most secondary school teachers in England and Wales, at least in public examinations at 16+, but it does require a profession knowledgeable in assessment techniques. At the moment, the profession acknowledges its relative lack of knowledge (see, for example, Schools Council, 1971) and, indeed, many teachers still prefer a totally external system of public examinations. This means that the examining boards and the Schools Council are, and will remain, constantly on the search for improved techniques of assessment that will minimize the backwash effect on the curriculum and teaching methods and that will enhance the technical efficiency of the examinations, without prejudicing the validity of the examination and the principle that the examining system should put the curriculum first (Schools Council, 1971). The place of criterion-referenced testing, as opposed to the current essentially norm-referenced testing, is also under debate as is the possibility of reporting attainment in terms of profiles rather than as a global grade (see, for example, Eggleston, 1974; White, 1974). White tells a cautionary tale in connection with profiles:

> "I always remember the delightful cartoon of many many years ago which showed a victim of the earlier part of the century with a sandwich board in Piccadilly, a man who had served both in the Boer War and the First World War. His sandwich board read, 'two wars, three wounds, four medals, one wife, six children—total 16'. There are some personal evaluations which can operate in very much the same way."

Reforms to the system of public examinations have invariably followed reforms in the structure of secondary education, as the Schools Council's paper, *Arguments for a Common System of Examining at 16+* (Schools Council, 1973a), demonstrates. As Professor Simon indicated, the move towards comprehensive education has led in turn to a consideration of the replacement of our present dual system by a common system of examining at 16+. Other possible reforms to the system of public examinations at both 17+ and 18+ are also in the air, but unfortunately there is no time to discuss them. However, many of the possible improvements to the system that I have been discussing have been carefully considered in Council publications (Schools Council, 1971; Schools Council, 1973b; Schools Council, 1973c) and, whether or not the structure is changed, public examinations will continue to evolve for the benefit of both pupils and teachers.

In conclusion, I therefore feel that, first, public examinations will continue for many years to come and, secondly, particularly if the trend is indeed towards improved techniques and more internal assessment, public examination will continue to have both a necessary and a valuable part to play in education.

## References

Board of Education. (1943). *Curriculum and Examinations in Secondary Schools*. The Norwood Report. London: HMSO.

Department of Education and Science. (1974). *1972 School Leavers, CSE and GCE.* Statistics of Education Vol. 2. London: HMSO.

Eggleston, J. F. (1974). Prediction, selection, description and choice. *Forum,* **16,** 61.

Entwistle, N. J. (1974). Personality and academic attainment. In *Educational Research in Britain 3.* Edited by H. J. Butcher and H. B. Pont. London: University of London Press.

Henrysson, S. (1964). The Swedish system of equalising marks. *Educational Research,* **6,** 156.

Hudson, L. (1964). Academic sheep and research goats. *New Society,* **108,** 9.

Jennings, A. H. (1974). Examining at 16+. In *Report of a Conference on Examinations and Assessment.* London: Chelsea College. Mimeo.

Ministry of Education. (1960). *Secondary School Examinations other than the GCE.* The Beloe Report. London: HMSO.

Morris, N. (1961). An historian's view of examinations. In *Examinations and English Education.* Edited by S. Wiseman. Manchester: Manchester University Press.

NFER School to University Research Unit. (1973). *The Prediction of Academic Success.* Slough: NFER.

Pidgeon, D. A. (1970). *Expectation and Pupil Performance.* Slough: NFER.

Rosenthal, R. and Jacobson, L. (1968). *Pygmalion in the Classroom.* New York: Holt, Rinehart and Winston.

Schools Council. (1971). *A Common System of Examining at 16+.* Schools Council Examinations Bulletin 23. London: Evans/Methuen Educational.

Schools Council. (1973a). *Arguments for a Common System of Examining at 16+.* London: Schools Council Publications.

Schools Council. (1973b). *16–19: Growth and Response. 2. Examination Structure.* Schools Council Working Paper 46. London: Evans/Methuen Educational.

Schools Council. (1973c). *Preparation for Degree Courses.* Schools Council Working Paper 47. London: Evans/Methuen Educational.

White W. M. (1974). Examinations in relation to the curriculum. In *Report of a Conference on Examinations and Assessment.* London: Chelsea College. Mimeo.

Wiseman, S. (1961). The efficiency of examinations. In *Examinations and English Education.* Edited by S. Wiseman. Manchester: Manchester University Press.

Yates, A. and Pidgeon, D. A. (1957). *Admission to Grammar Schools.* London: Newnes for NFER.

# The Galton Lecture 1974: The Docimological Dilemma: Quality Control or Quantity Surveying?

## W. H. G. ARMYTAGE

*Division of Education, University of Sheffield, Sheffield, England*

"A question that now continually arises is this: a youth is a candidate for permanent employment, his present personal qualifications are known, but how will he turn out in later years? The objections to competitive examinations are notorious, in that they give undue prominence to youths whose receptive faculties are quick, and whose intellects are precocious. They give no indication of the directions in which the health, character, and intellect of the youth will change through the development, in their due course, of ancestral tendencies that are latent in youth, but will manifest themselves in after life. Examinations deal with the present, not with the future, although it is in the future of the youth that we are especially interested."

Sir Francis Galton (1928).

The most Chinese among all the nest of boxes so delicately raised in the quest of equality of opportunity is that of equity of assessment.

It is, or should be, the calibrator by which all advances towards equality of opportunity are measured. And as universities and polytechnics are increasingly perceived as part of a system of talent identification rather than as selection agencies or boosters of industrial or agrarian productivity, so the techniques of identifying and certifying this talent are of concern to everyone (Psacharopoulos, 1973; Taubman and Wales, 1973).

However arcane, such techniques are capable of some evaluation if only at the level of "what University?" or "what subject?". As the innovating Master of a fictitious Cambridge college was recently depicted asking his Bursar "When did we last get a first?" "In 1956" said the Bursar. The Master raised his eyes to heaven. "In Geography" said the Bursar, rubbing salt into the wound (Sharpe, 1974).

I mention Cambridge since its mathematics Tripos represented examinationism at its apogee. Indeed, up to 1907, candidates used to be assessed like racehorses, even to the extent of bookies from nearby Newmarket taking odds on the favourites. One such was J. H. Grace. Another, whose actual name has not been revealed by the Royal Society memoir from which I take this story, was seen to stumble (I believe he took a girl on the river). This stumble so concerned his backers that they pinned on his door a verse from a hymn more familiar in 1895 than now. It ran:

> "Work, as if on that alone
> Hung the issue of that day,
> Pray that Grace may be sent down,
> Work and Pray."

J. H. Grace was actually bracketed second wrangler in 1895, was elected to the Royal Society thirteen years later and subsequently had a breakdown.

Like hymns, examinations have a sort of agryphotic purpose in that they keep students awake. Hence the use of the term docimology in my title, for it was used to describe the science of assessing drugs. It was also used to describe the science of assaying metals and, so by a kind of Platonic analogy, might well be used to describe the art of assessing the mettle of students. Karl Pearson would, I'm sure, have approved for, as you know, he held that a fundamental part of logic was what he called 'the study and right use of language, the clear definition, and, if needful, invention of terms' (Pearson, 1935). Docimology was indeed prescribed as a necessary component in the training of all teachers by M. Toussaint at the *ad hoc* conference of European Ministers of Education on 12–14 September 1967 (Haigh, 1970).

He did so because the term was familiar on the continent, having been used by Binet's successor at the Laboratory of Experimental Psychology at the Sorbonne, Henri Pieron, who realised that there was a science behind academic assessment. He appropriated the term in his *Études docimologiques sur le perfectionnement des examens* (1934). Thirty years later his conviction that the examiner played as great, if not a greater part than the examinee in the determination of marks was tersely and cogently expressed in *Examens et docimologie* (Pieron, 1963). This was, of course, the year in which the Robbins Committee, in spite of recommending "a radical review of courses as a whole", shied away from the question as to whether existing university entrance or exit tests made possible what is called "a just assessment of the ability of candidates" by pointing out that an answer would involve "intricate research and would involve complex questions" beyond their competence (Robbins, 1963). It did however call attention to the wide distribution of firsts, pointing out for instance that only 4% got firsts in history as opposed to 14% in mathematics. Two years later Robbins chaired a Eugenics Society symposium on 30 September 1965, and he confessed himself in agreement with nearly every criticism of existing entry and exit tests in higher education made on that occasion by Dr Liam Hudson, Dr James Drever and Mrs Jean Floud. He threw in, by way of an aside, his opinion that the school report seemed to him to be as good a way of choosing people as any other (Meade and Parkes, 1966).

In a sense he could be said to have brought into the open the dilemma between quality control and quantity assessment by basing his recommendations for expansion of universities on social demand. Some answers and further questions were supplied by an issue of the *Universities Quarterly* (1967). Many universities (some through their staff student committees) conducted enquiries: that conducted by my own in 1969 revealed the not surprising fact that students want to be better assessed all round, assignments of various kinds being included in the ultimate assessment (Orton, 1969). The enquiry currently being conducted at the University of Edinburgh has already uncovered degrees of awareness to cues from staff about examinations (which virtually constitute a hidden curriculum) and has coined the categories the "cue-seekers", the "cue-conscious" and the "cue-deaf", to resolve the degrees of alertness to possible questions (Miller and Parlett, 1974). At another university, Leeds, one of the professors categorically stated that there is "without doubt, a case for a radical revision of the present degree examinations" (Layton, 1968). Students in fifteen British universities also made it quite plain to the Select Committee on Education and Science in 1969 that existing systems of assessment were not proof against arbitrary decisions and inefficiency, and exercised a detrimental influence over the courses. "Failure" rates were also seen to vary from university to university and within universities from course to course. Nor were arrangement for remedying such failures by re-sitting seen to be either rational or uniform (Select Committee on Education and Science, 1969). *The World Year Book of Education for 1969* was built round the editorial claim that:

"Profound scepticism of traditional examination systems has not yet been matched by the collective creativity needed to devise tests which are not only valid and reliable, nationally, but are capable of assessing competence in an international setting." (Lauwerys, 1969.)

"*Where*" actually published a shopping list of universities in March 1971 order of their award of firsts. Kent was the "best buy" with 17% of its honours graduates getting firsts in 1968 as opposed to Keele where only 4·9% got firsts.

To clear the air the Vice Chancellors and Principals convened a joint conference with the Association of University Teachers to discuss the problem (Drever, 1969). The NUS had a conference on Assessment in 1970 and in 1973 joined with the AUT, the ATTI and the ATCDE in the Nuffield Foundation's Working Session on Assessment in June 1973. Whilst all this was taking place, others were wrestling with what might be called the post-Swann neurosis: i.e. the fear that their discipline would be threatened and standards would be lowered if they were forced to hawk their wares in some Pippardian type of super-market (Hinton, 1973). Further perturbants were the "new subjects" in the "new universities" which pioneered new methods of assessment. Thus the head of the Department of Architectural Planning and Urban Studies at Aston publicly suggested that every classification should bear a date stamp and an expiry date (Swann, 1968), whilst a Reader in Statistics at the University of London suggested that honours examinations were "rituals rather than efforts at educational measurement" (Hajnal, 1972). All this indicated that the movement was not so much to abolish assessment as to improve it. But, the lively and energetic disputants, as might be expected, raised so many "more questions than answers . . . about the road to improvement" that Dr Halsey confessed that his travels along that road encountered "endemic fog" (Halsey, 1974).

My object in this lecture is to indicate certain features in the macro-climate that might help dispel that fog. True, some fog—pettifog especially—seems endemic in higher education. It might almost be justified as necessary to elicit groping skills. For as Herbert Crovitz remarked in a stimulating essay entitled *Galton's Walk: Methods for the Analysis of Thinking, Intelligence and Creativity*, "groping is one price a finite creature has to pay in searching according to a method" (Crovitz, 1970). Yet as we grope, we can hear danger signals which should enable us to modify our courses.

The first noise comes from the Civil Service, which has long exercised a major influence over both university and school examinations. Since these examinations began candidates have sought the services of "coaches" and "crammers", so much so that by 1905 the Master of

Balliol was complaining that coaches rather than the colleges commanded the portals of Whitehall (Mackail, 1925). Some seventeen years later, when the introduction of English as a Tripos subject was being discussed at Cambridge, the opinion of the Senior Civil Service Commissioners was sought before action was taken (Tillyard, 1958). The result was that supplementary cramming virtually disappeared, and the Grade I Civil Service examination had become, for the really clever boy, a sequential hurdle to a first.

But after World War II, those academic type examinations (now known as Method I) were supplemented by, and have now been virtually displaced by, what one might call the more docimologically based Method II. This owed much to the War Office Selection Boards. The change seems to have accelerated five trends that bear on the subject of this symposium. First: Oxford and Cambridge no longer provide the majority of candidates, only $58 \cdot 7\%$ of the total came from these two universities in 1968 as opposed to an average of $88 \cdot 1\%$ in 1959–63. Second: most candidates seem to be coming from LEA schools, and though these did not form a a majority of the successful candidates in 1968, they comprised $41 \cdot 3\%$ of the successes as opposed to $28 \cdot 6\%$ over the years 1959–63. Third: there has been a rise in the percentage of candidates studying economics, politics, science, technology and mathematics at the expense of those studying history, classics, modern languages and English. Fourth: there has been a small decrease in the proportion of successful candidates with firsts. Fifth: though the social background of candidates has not substantially altered, there has been some decrease in the proportion of successful candidates from the Registrar General's Groups 1 and 2 (Fry, 1969).

These trends were identified in 1969 by a Committee of Inquiry into Method II chaired by Mr J. G. W. Davies. His committee distinguished between the intellectual quality of a candidate "for the work of the Administrative Civil Service" as opposed to what it called "the academic point of view". It also recommended that holders of first class honours or further degrees should no longer be exempted from the Qualifying Examination, which should itself be radically overhauled.

In view of the great influence that the examinations for Grade I of the Civil Service once more have on these for university degrees it is perhaps worth quoting at length one of the Committee's proposals:

"Our proposal is that the most effective of the papers in the present examination, i.e. the English summary and the figure-based descriptive exercise, should be retained. The remainder should be scrapped and in their place we recommend a battery of objective tests containing both verbal and non-verbal elements . . . The Statistical Inferences Test or something akin to it should be included at this stage . . . We should also like to see an essay included . . . to give the candidate free rein to display a flow of ideas and fertility of mind. We know that there is a general interest among psychologists and educationalists in the development of tests to this end." (Davies, 1969.)

And what of the professions that have done so much to foster examinations? Here an equally bracing wind has blown from the Monopolies Commission. After scrutinizing the relevance of existing tests of competence to the services rendered by some 130 professions to the public, it reported that some of them, in attempting to pull themselves up to the standard of others, have actually demanded a standard of intellectual attainment far beyond that required of their practitioners in day-to-day work. The Monopolies Commission detected:

"A risk that those who are already qualified will be slow to recognize that the kind of test that was appropriate when they entered the profession has ceased to be appropriate because the services demanded from the profession have changed".

It also doubted whether tests of competence, however appropriate in respect of current knowledge and ability, could adequately safeguard the level of future performance. Conversely, whilst acknowledging the need for a severe and relevant test, the Monopolies Commission suggested that the quality and availability of the services offered by various professions would be improved if such professions delegated some of their work to others by establishing further specialist and differential qualifications (The Monopolies Commission, 1970). A third inquiry, this time into that most conservative profession, the law, has also made some interesting observations on what has been, so far, the main route to such qualifications—the examination. It defined what it called "the ineradicable tendency" of examinations, "to divert students from learning all they can to equip themselves for the future" in order to concentrate on memorizing information. It realized that examinations dictated "both the nature of the courses and the method of instruction". Its conclusions are worth quoting in full:

"The aim should be to test the ability of candidates to apply their legal knowledge to practical problems over a fairly wide field. Candidates should be presented with detailed factual situations (with irrelevant facts stated as well as relevant ones) and be required to advise or to draft the requisite legal documents. So far as possible they should be allowed to use the relevant statutes, text-books and precedent books rather than be made to commit the professional sin of relying on fallible memory." (Ormrod, 1970).

It also commended:

"Individual assignments undertaken in the students own time".

This coincides remarkably with the views of one of the newest professions of all: computing. For the British Computing Society complained to the Select Committee on Science and Technology that

"Nearly all our educational activities behave as if the individual is going to work alone. This goes right through to research work in the universities, whereas computing is an example of the kind of thing which is now becoming more widespread in science and technology and the loner has only a limited contribution to make." (Select Committee on Science and Technology, 1971.)

Computing looks like moving up after petroleum and automobiles, to become the world's third largest industry. In Britain it is almost certain to involve 10% of the working population by 1980 (Select Committee on Science and Technology, 1971). With the most advanced independent software and services industry in Europe, and with the Hoskyns Group forecasting that the growth of the data processing industry in the seventies will be primarily in the service area, Britain needs all the non-loners it can get.

Use of the computer has already, through UCCA, done much to equalize university recruitment, by making the choice of university "less crucial and cumulatively less consequential" enabling universities to "compete for talent on roughly equal terms" (Morris, K. H., 1969). Its diagnostic powers are being daily extended. Electronic screening centres are now in full swing in the United States. Above all it is quietly revolutionizing the docimological role of the teacher enabling him to be seen as "a manager trained in the skills necessary to counsel, plan and co-ordinate as well as contribute to the teacher learning process" (Morris, A., 1974). The NUS have told the Expenditure Committee that they favour the computer matching of jobs and graduates, and have themselves initiated a pilot computer placement service (House of Commons, 1973a).

One effective dispersant of fog is wind, and the ever lowering temperature of those now blowing from the Treasury and from a new committee of the House of Commons known as the Expenditure

Committee are eliciting a clearer view of priorities. They seem to have caused some hitherto specialist university departments to huddle up into divisions in order to make their staff student ratios more respect- able. Even those who resent being brigaded with their institutional cognates, now have to develop a taxonomy of their objectives a little more tightly argued, and much less indulgently heard, than the traditional inaugural lecture. So the cold winds may be blowing to some good purpose if they ruffle such a taxonomy into existence, for we have Professor Jevons's word for it that apart from some uninspired quoting of Bloom no such taxonomy is at present widely used in the context of higher education (Jevons and Turner, 1972). Such a taxonomy might also help counter the opinions put forward by those leading industrial executives in the newspapers, who are currently stressing that three years in the Army can "equal" three years at a university because the Army allegedly offers experience in making decisions and accepting the responsibility for them.

Since 1971 this new committee of the House of Commons (the Expenditure Committee) has been busy and active. It has suggested that universities, polytechnics, colleges of education and colleges of further education should be more closely linked under a Higher Education Commission informed by a National Manpower Council and working through a National Careers Advisory Service (House of Commons, 1972). Into this framework a case has been made for the inclusion of Adult Education (Rhodes, 1973). It has also recom- mended that all post-graduate work should be monitored by a National Advisory Council (House of Commons, 1973b; Department of Education and Science, 1973). Its most recent recommendation—a proper system of allowances for the post-sixteen year olds (House of Commons, 1974) is an indication that it is serious about giving them greater independence: an independence which has now become legally absolute at eighteen. Despite sixth form power have we done much to remedy the Hale Committee's complaint that "many, perhaps most", of the "students on entry to the university" hardly got beyond the stage of taking their opinions from authority and expect "to find the 'right' answers to all questions in a textbook" (Hale, 1964). This is not surprising, for in the diverse sixth forms of today "close supervision" might, as Dr G. W. Miller pointed out, "be necessary to prevent any possible deterioration in morale extending downwards to lower forms". "If such fears are justified", he goes on "they would support the case for separate sixth forms or junior colleges" (Miller, G. W. 1920).

Another fog clearer is the Dip.HE for discussions about it are transforming the method and metaphor of assessment. The flow diagrams of the quality controller now replace the chilling numeracy of the quantity surveyor. And in this the influence of the National Union of Students is also visible, for in 1961, long before Lord James suggested the Dip.HE, they suggested such a two-year course in their evidence to the Robbins Committee. Now, in 1974, they have contributed an opinion to the debate on quality control versus quantity surveying by publishing *Pro-Profiles*, not as an expression of the Union's views but in their words, as a contribution to an "urgently called for" debate.

This describes profiles—assessment or descriptive—as "offering an opportunity to fashion a mode of presenting the results of formal assessment which is more informative, less distorting and less misleading". It also sees profiles as "complementary to contemporary moves towards flexible course structure and multiform methods of assessment". Lastly it claims that a complex profile will "liberate educational institutions from the need to relate every course option and variety of test to a simple standard measure"; thereby removing restraints on courses which cannot be assessed in the single grade or class of the whole subject (Klug, 1974).

The main guide-lines of the Dip.HE have been drawn by a trans-binary group composed of representatives of the CNAA, the CVCP and the Open University, first published in May 1973 they were revised in July 1973. CNAA has also formed a Dip.HE validation group under the Principal of the Berkshire College of Education. This College is about to mount one trial run Dip.HE. Another, influenced by the growing American University practice, the "learning contract", is starting with some sixty-seven students at the North East London Polytechnic this coming term and is also being monitored by CNAA.

The NELP course involves mutual discussion about the skills a student hopes to acquire at the end of the course and how these can best be achieved. Such discussions may well last for about six weeks and such skills to be acquired will, it is hoped, emerge from the discovery, organization and presentation of solutions to problems posed by the student. These "learning contracts" are being used at the University of Illinois, and represent an advance on the traditional type of American supermarket type modules. One might call it a salad (as opposed to a sandwich) course for those who are still green in judgement.

The flow diagrams now being seriously drawn at conferences of the Regional Advisory Councils have brought other awards into the arena of discussion. How, for instance, will the Dip.HE relate to the HND which is already a recognized staging post to the B.Sc as well as an award in its own right. Will the more volatile components of the age cohort flow to the Dip.HE leaving the heavier fractions in the HND pipeline? And will this affect the present status of the HND which the quantity surveyors think is only half a degree whereas the Dip.HE might be thought to be two thirds? Will the monitoring role of the CNAA—our first recognized academic quality control institution—lead it to initiate more transbinary discussions on transcript transfers: already growing rapidly as open university graduates present themselves for higher degrees in other institutions?

These three questions are only some that arise from the appearance of the modular, accumulative and combinatorial, Dip.HE: the first real flow process award. But it has yet to be generally accepted by the Civil Service and by other professions. Has accountancy, for long in thrall to the correspondence colleges, given a lead in accepting it as a necessary preliminary of professional training (Solomons, 1974)? Might it also become the first common European award, since French universities start their two year Diploma des Etudes Universitaires Generales this year? If the proposals of the Carnegie Commission of the United States, as outlined in *Less Time More Options* (1971) are implemented, the Dip.HE may well win a transatlantic acceptance too.

This is why the suggestion of the Expenditure Commission of the House of Commons that universities, polytechnics, colleges of education and colleges of further education might be more closely linked under a Higher Education Commission informed by a National Manpower Council and working through a National Careers Advisory Service has a basic logic. So has the Labour Party's inclusion of Adult Education.

But the Dip.HE is a novelty, and as F. M. Cornford sagely observed in his little classic *Microcosmographia Academica* (1908):

"Every public action which is not customary, either is wrong or, if it is right, is a dangerous precedent. It follows therefore that nothing can be done for the first time".

So I commend the significance of Sherlock Holmes, who you remember spent his time at the university not in studying the Copernican theory nor in reading Carlyle but in working out his own little methods of thought (Doyle, 1952).

These "own little methods" have made Sherlock Holmes the fictive model of heurism, for his greatest enemy was the crammer—Professor Moriarty—a former professor at one of Britain's smaller universities. Now I would put it to you that if Holmes is the father of heurism,

Dr Watson is the father of the profile. How many of you realize that Watson, knowing only too well that Holmes was "as sensitive to flattery on the score of his art as any girl could be of her beauty", compiled a twelve point profile, aptly entitled *Sherlock Holmes—his limits*.

"1. Knowledge of Literature—Nil.
2. Knowledge of Philosophy—Nil.
3. Knowledge of Astronomy—Nil.
4. Knowledge of Politics—Feeble.
5. Knowledge of Botany—Variable. Well up in Belladonna, opium and poisons generally. Knows nothing of practical gardening.
6. Knowledge of Geology—Practical, but limited. Tells at a glance different soils from each other. After walks has shown me splashes upon his trousers, and told me by their colour and consistency in what part of London he had received them.
7. Knowledge of Chemistry—Profound.
8. Knowledge of Anatomy—Accurate, but unsystematic.
9. Knowledge of Sensational Literature—Immense. He appears to know every detail of every horror perpetrated in the century.
10. Plays the violin well.
11. Is an expert singlestick player, boxer and swordsman.
12. Has a good practical knowledge of British law." (Doyle, 1952).

I wish all degree certificates or references for that matter, were as informative.

Both Holmes and Watson were practitioners of mutual ranking, a practice also glancingly endorsed by the Committee on the Method II examination for the Administrative Grade of the Civil Service as providing "some evidence about the impact of a candidate upon his contemporaries and his ability to size up his fellows" (Doyle, 1952).

But to conclude. My argument is that there seems to be a trend towards equity of assessment, an equity which may be reacting reciprocally with the push to equalize opportunity. And the push for equity derives not a little of its impetus from the middle classes. For whilst the university entry chances of children of manual workers have improved during the 1960s from one in six to one in four (Glennerster, 1972), middle class children educated at independent schools, have been streaming into the polytechnics—so much so that in at least one of them (Enfield) they constitute a majority (Donaldson, 1971). So here we have, at the tertiary level, the phenomenon which occurred at the secondary level in 1957, when the middle class component of the 1946–47 bulge fouled the quantity surveyors' 11+ barrier, and made comprehensive education a CASE rather than a cause. Moreover the increasing fertility of that class, reflected in the U-shaped class fertility curve of the 1960s, also looks like bringing about a greater equalization of awards, and ensuring that more does not mean worse by supporting some system of quality control.

So just as St Michael has become the patron saint of a good shirt, he may become a tutorial as well as a tutelary, saint of a good academic gown, even though his name will not be invoked on the banks of the Cam and of the Isis.

But I have hopes, especially if Cambridge could remember there is what Cornford would call a precedent for treating a good Dip.HE as the equivalent of Part I of their tripos. For in the early days of my own university and those of Nottingham, before either were chartered to award their own degrees, Cambridge used to accord "affiliate" status to our students. This enabled those who had spent two years of satisfactory study in either institution to go up for Part II of a Tripos— a real flow award. Some such arrangements are already eventuating elsewhere. Perhaps if the age cohort were to stabilize after its present shrinkage (for it has dropped by 25% in the last ten years from 876,000 to just over 700,000) we might go forward on lines adumbrated in the U68 Commission in Sweden, providing a post Dip.HE training in technology, administration and economics, or medicine and social work, or teaching and cultural work and information (Allmäna, 1973; Jantsch, 1969). Some such arrangements would, it seems, have to be made if present employment trends continue and the numbers working in the public service increase (at present they constitute one in three of the workforce). To these should be added many others working in the private civil services of the great oligopolies such as Shell, ICI, Unilever which oblige engineers and scientists to undertake a wide variety of jobs, to be problem-oriented and to respond to incentives to avoid obsolescence. And even outside these public and private civil services minor firms are buying places on retraining courses, where case study, role simulation, and use of the computer figure prominently in the curriculum.

The second trend is that computer installations are increasing at the rate of 40% per annum. So such retraining will only be effective if it ministers to those quickened (as opposed to deadened) to problem-solving procedures involving quantitative techniques *and* qualitative judgements. This, it seems, is what the Committee on Scientific Man-power meant when it called upon the Committee of Vice-Chancellors and Principals in 1968 to initiate what it called "a radical rethinking of the educational process". Any such rooting about the groves of academe (if one can imagine vice-chancellors undertaking such an inelegant task) would reveal that the real curriculum is governed by the system of assessment. And so it should be for, by proper validation, each individual student is helped thereby to acquire a better sense of his or her identity and if necessary can cool out (or stoke up) his or her career aspirations.

## References

Allmäna, F. (1973). *Higher Education: Proposals by the Swedish 1968 Educational Commission.* Summary. Stockholm.

Bloom, B. S., Hastings, J. T. and Madaus, G. F. (1971). *Handbook on Formative and Summative Evaluation of Student Learning.* New York: McGraw Hill.

Caves, R. E. and Associates. (1968). *Britain's Economic Prospects*, pp. 332 and 422–425. Washington: Brookings Institute.

Committee of Inquiry. (1969). *The Method II System of Selection for the Administrative Class of the Home Civil Service*, p. 84. Chairman: Mr J. G. W. Davies. Cmnd. 4156. London, HMSO.

Committee on Higher Education. (1963a). *Higher Education.* Report of the Committee Appointed by the Prime Minister under the Chairmanship of Lord Robbins, paras 255 and 524. Cmnd. 2154. London: HMSO.

Committee on Higher Education. (1963b). *Higher Education.* Report of the Committee Appointed by the Prime Minister under the Chairmanship of Lord Robbins, pp. 145–147. Cmnd. 2154–11. London: HMSO.

Committee on Legal Education. (1971). *Report of the Committee on Legal Education*, para, 165. Chairman: Mr Justice Ormrod. Cmnd. 4595. London: HMSO.

Committee on Teaching Methods. (1964). *Report of the Committee on Teaching Methods.* Chairman: Sir Edward Hale. London: HMSO.

Crovitz, H. F. (1970). *Galton's Walk: Methods for the Analysis of Thinking, Intelligence and Creativity*, pp. 151–152. London: Harper and Row.

Department of Education and Science Expenditure Committee. (1973). *Government Observations on Report on Further and Higher Education.* Cmnd. 5368. London: HMSO.

Donaldson, L. (1971). Social class and the polytechnics. *Higher Education Review.* Autumn.

Doyle, Sir A. Conan. (1952a). The scarlet runner. In *Sherlock Holmes. His Adventures, Memoirs, Return.* London: John Murray.

Doyle, Sir A. Conan. (1952b). *Sherlock Holmes. His Adventures, Memoirs, Return*, pp. 379 and 539. London: John Murray.

Doyle, Sir A. Conan. (1952c). *Sherlock Holmes. His Adventures, Memoirs, Return*, p. 17. London: John Murray.

Drever, J. (Chairman). (1969). *Assessment of Undergraduate Performance.* Conference convened by the Committee of Vice Chancellors and Principals and the Association of University Teachers. March. London: Committee of Vice Chancellors and Principals of the Universities of the UK.

*An Evaluation Guidebook.* (1972). Los Angeles: The Instructional Objectives Exchange.

Fry, G. K. (1969). *Statesmen in Disguise: The Changing Role of the Administrative Class of the British Home Civil Service 1853–1966.* London: MacMillan.

Galton, Sir F. (1928). *Inquiries into Human Faculty and its Development*, pp. 211–212. London: J. M. Dent and Sons, Ltd.

Glennerster, H. (1972). *Labour and Inequality.* London: The Fabian Society.

Haigh, A. (1970). *A Ministry of Education for Europe*, p. 116. London: George G. Harrap.

Hajnal, J. (1972). *The Student Trap. A Critique of University and Sixth Form*. Harmondsworth, Middlesex: Penguin Books.

Halsey, A. H. (1974). *The Times Higher Educational Supplement*. 2 August.

Hinton, D. (1973). A teamwork graduate profile to replace the grading sieve. *The Times Higher Educational Supplement*. 20 April.

House of Commons Expenditure Committee. (1972). *Report from the Expenditure Committee, together with Minutes of Evidence taken before the Education and Arts Sub-Committee in Session 1971–72. Appendices and Index. Session 1972–73. Further and Higher Education*. Volumes I, II and III, 48, i–iii. London: HMSO.

House of Commons Expenditure Committee. (1973a). *Seventh Report of the Expenditure Committee Session 1972–73. Employment Services and Training*, 214, i–iii. London: HMSO.

House of Commons Expenditure Committee. (1973b). *Third Report of the Expenditure Committee, together with the Minutes of the Evidence taken before the Education and Arts Sub-Committee in Session 1972–73. Session 1973–74, Postgraduate Education*. Volumes 1 and 2, 96, i, ii. London: HMSO.

House of Commons Expenditure Committee. (1974). Expenditure Committee (Education and Arts Sub-Committee) Minutes of Evidence 4 February 1974. Session 1973–74. *Further Developments in Higher and Further Education*. London: HMSO.

House of Commons Select Committee. (1969). *Report from the Select Committee on Education and Science: Session 1968–69. Student Relations*. Vol. 1, paras 391–398. London: HMSO.

House of Commons Select Committee. (1971). *Fourth Report from the Select Committee on Science and Technology, Session 1970–71. The Prospects for the United Kingdom Computer Industry in the 1970s*, Vol. 1, p. xi, Vol 2, p. 1587. London: HMSO.

Jantsch, E. (1969). Integrative Planning for the joint systems of society and technology: the emerging role of the university. *Ekistics*, **28**, 169. December.

Jevons, F. R. and Turner, H. D. (Editors) (1972). *What Kinds of Graduates do we Need?* London: Oxford University Press.

Klug, B. (1974). *Pro-Profiles*, p. 37. London: National Union of Students.

Labour Party. (1973). *Higher and Further Education: Report of a Labour Party Study Group Opposition Green Paper*. Chairman: Geoffrey Rhodes. London: Labour Party.

Lauwerys, J. A. (1969). Education and examinations. In *World Yearbook of Education for 1969*, p. 16. London: Evans Brothers.

Layton, D. (Editor) (1968). *University Teaching in Transition*, p. 140. Edinburgh: Oliver and Boyd.

Mackail, J. W. (1925). *James Leigh Strachan-Davidson*, p. 191. Oxford: Clarendon Press.

Meade, J. E. and Parkes, A. S. (Editors) (1966). *Genetics and Environmental Factors in Human Ability*, p. 101. Edinburgh: Oliver and Boyd.

Miller, C. M. L. and Parlett, M. (1974). *Up to the Mark: A Study of the Examination Game*, p. 494. London: The Society for Research into Higher Education.

Miller, G. W. (1920). *Success, Failure and Wastage in Higher Education: An Overview of its Problems Derived from Research and Theory*, pp. 188–189. London: George G. Harrap.

Monopolies Commission. (1970). *A Report on the General effect of the Public Interest of Certain Restrictive Practices so as they Prevail in Relation to the Supply of Professional Services*. Part I: *The Report*; Part II: The Appendices. Cmnd. 4463, para. 62. London: HMSO.

Morris, A. (1974). Flexibility and tenured academic. *Higher Education Review 6, 2, 21.*

Morris, K. H. (1969). *The Sixth Form and College Entrance,* p. 15. London: Routledge and Kegan Paul.

Orton, F. J. (Editor) (1969). *Assessment of Students.* University of Sheffield.

Pearson, K. (1935). *The Grammar of Science.* London: Dent.

Pieron, H. (1963). *Examens et Docimologie.* Paris: Presses Universitaires de France.

Popham, W. J. (1971). *Criterion-referenced Measurement: An Introduction.* New Jersey: Englewood Cliffs.

Psacharopoulos, G. (1973). *Return to Education: An International Comparison.* New York, Amsterdam and London: Elsevier Scientific Publishing Co.

Rosenthal, R. and Jacobson, L. (1968). *Pygmalion in the Classroom. Teacher Expectation and Pupil's Intellectual Development.* London: Holt, Rinehart and Winston.

Sharpe, T. (1974). *Porterhouse Blue,* p. 26. London: Secker and Warburg.

Solomons, D. (1974). *Prospectus for a Profession.* London: Gee and Co.

Swann, M. M. (Chairman) (1968a). *The Flow into Employment of Scientists, Engineers and Technologists. Report of the Working Group on Manpower and Scientific Growth,* paras 128–130. Cmnd. 3760. London: HMSO.

Swann, M. M. (Chairman) (1968b). Outline of a proposal for reorganising university education. As Annexe to *The Flow into Employment of Scientists, Engineers and Technologists. Report of the Working Group on Manpower for Scientific Growth.* Cmnd. 3760.

Taubman, P. F. and Wales, T. F. (1973). Higher education, mental ability and screening. *Journal of Political Economy,* **LXXXI**, 1, 28–55.

Tillyard, E. M. W. (1958). *The Muse Unchained: An Intimate Account of the Revolution in English Studies at Cambridge,* p. 52. London: Bowes and Bowes.

Todd, J. A. (1958). John Hilton Grace 1873–1955. *Biographical Memoirs of Fellows of the Royal Society,* **4,** 93.

# International Differences in Higher Education

## ARTHUR HEARNDEN

*Department of Comparative Education,*
*University of London Institute of Education, London, England*

The hundred or so reports published by the Carnegie Commission in the United States and the recent deliberations of the Conference of European Rectors at Bologna on the theme "European Universities 1975–1985" are just a few of the more specular breakers in the current flood tide of academic introspection. By comparison, the disturbances caused in the United Kingdom by the Robbins episode a decade ago were those of a quiet Mediterranean creek. It would seem that never before has there been such widespread and obsessive concern with the present problems and future shape of higher education. The superficial manifestation of the turbulence is the presence somewhere off the academic coastline of a school of ungainly mammals, described as comprehensive universities, disporting themselves in a manner that to many in the academic world is either alarming or indecent or both. But the appearance of these unfamiliar creatures is merely a symptom of a deeper ferment as higher education is confronted with social and economic forces of unusual magnitude.

Previous major stages of development in education have on the whole been characterized by a buoyant feeling that a new phase of human progress is being celebrated. One thinks for example of the great principles of *Lehrfreiheit* and *Lernfreiheit* that inspired Wilhelm von Humboldt's creation of the University of Berlin; or the stirring words with which the Robbins expansion was endorsed. It may of course be that an atmosphere of crusading optimism is more obvious in retrospect. But even allowing for the natural submergence with time of contemporary carpings, the new situation does seem somewhat different. The Carnegie Commission could observe that

95

"higher education is making a first descent into a strange world where future prospects are not thought to be limitless".

When such a sobering understatement emerges from the United States of all places, is it any wonder that in other countries less accustomed to feeling that the world is at their feet, the advent of something called "mass higher education" appears not so much a vision as a spectre.

In a recent interview Sir Alan Bullock reduced the current criticisms of universities to two main themes (*The Observer*, 1973). The first was that they are not mass institutions and he pointed to the school of thought that would like to see them accessible to all who desire higher education and to see their activities conducted at levels and by methods appropriate to the range of ability that this implies. As well as this populist challenge he identified a second criticism which sees university education as too academic and too little concerned with the practical application of knowledge, a school of thought which accepts the notion of an elite but maintains that it should be of a kind appropriate to the needs of a managerial and technological society.

Now the criticisms have mainly been directed in a rather loose way at what we might call the traditional universities rather than at higher education as a whole. But there are after all technological universities and polytechnics in the United Kingdom, *Technische Hochschulen* and *Fachhochschulen* in the Federal Republic of Germany, *grandes ecoles* and *instituts universitaires de technologie* in France. As far as relevance is concerned, none of these could be accused of neglecting the obligation to turn out the qualified practitioners needed to make a complex society function. And as they are expanding they can surely be expected to meet the demands of the employment market.

This is all very true but with the exception of the *grandes ecoles* they are not the elite institutions most sought after by school leavers. We know very well that it is the traditional universities to which the magnetic elite label still attaches, and they retain the aura of luxury institutions, adornments to society rather than servants of it. Competition for scarce resources has however made their justification less and less easy; and as a result the idea gets about that they may be providing more adornment than the State can afford. As higher education has become a massive sector of economic planning, and economic planning has had to come to terms with budget reductions, so the pressure has grown for the universities to become integrated into the total system rather than remain privileged autonomous havens at one remove from it. The demand that they should be subjected to cost-benefit analysis expresses a sentiment that finds a sympathetic ear among hard-pressed taxpayers. And so, just as was earlier the case with secondary schools, so at the tertiary level the economic pressures to rationalize and get value for money join up with the social pressures to democratize and do away with elite treatment in the common call to "go comprehensive". Pursued to their conclusion, the arguments find no place for a distinctive university sector within the domain of higher education as a whole.

In our own United Kingdom context those whose task it is to predict and make decisions about higher education are in a relatively fortunate position. Having been party to the massive exercise devoted to the digestion of the recent past to which I referred earlier, they are highly informed about the nature of the arguments, and they have the further advantage that they can survey the consequences of acting on these arguments that are evident in other countries. They have witnessed the convulsions; what is there to be learnt from them?

To illuminate the argument about relevance we can look to the socialist world where university students are not allowed to forget that their studies are designed to be of practical benefit to society, where the requirements of the State determine what they should read and how they will subsequently be employed. There does remain in Eastern Europe the distinction between universities and polytechnics with which we are familiar but as Professor Suchodolski of Warsaw, writing in the World Yearbook of Education for 1971–72, points out it has become increasingly controversial; in point of fact universities

"are no longer places where eminent professors lecture on what interests them and students choose such lectures as they prefer . . . they have become similar to all other 'schools' and many people still recall with regret the loss of their former character as places of free scholarship".

Clearly however, this is the price paid for the total integration of the universities into the planned economy of the State.

In practical terms we are talking about the exercise of power and authority. To quote Suchodolski once again, the universities

"are no longer the autonomous corporate bodies which they used to be. University authorities are appointed by the Minister of Education and the appointment of a teacher or a professor also rests with the Minister although an opinion and a proposal from the university are required".

By controlling recruitment in this way, the State is also in a position to ensure that its objectives are carried out via the curriculum. Broadly speaking, higher education is expected to pursue to a conclusion the polytechnical instruction which permeates the school system from kindergarten to upper secondary level and of which the *leitmotiv* is that theory cannot be divorced from practice nor education from life. Though the precise form may differ from country to country this is the fundamental thesis that underlies higher education practice in the socialist world.

The most awesome example in this vein comes from China with the reports of how since the Cultural Revolution students have been drawn from the ranks of industrial and agricultural workers and soldiers, how they engage alternately in study and manual labour, how the old-style examination papers have been replaced by a requirement to give lectures to labour groups and to produce reports on experiences in manual work, and finally how after graduation they return to their factories, farms and military units to put their university training to practical use. According to the Chinese press agency, the reports on practical experience which are used for assessment are better than the old-style examination papers because they deal with urgent problems and research done under real conditions (*The Irish Times*, 1974).

The example of China is of course an extreme one but it serves to point up the dilemmas that arise when the State exerts pressure to make the work of institutions "relevant". To seek such relevance is a fairly straightforward matter if there is a prevailing ideological orthodoxy according to which it can be defined and an authority and power structure through which it can be enforced. There is then no problem, for instance, in doing away with a number of chairs of theology, replacing them with chairs of, say, political economy and administration, and making the corresponding changes in the number of student places available in these two fields. Indeed this appears as the natural way to subordinate academic freedom to the national interest. On the other hand, in a Western pluralistic context there could in theory be a massive revival of interest in theology among the student population, the universities would feel obliged to cater for it and the State would not really be in a position to suppress it. The point is not so much that academic freedom would be triumphing over the national interest but that universities would be taking a hand in interpreting the national interest in this particular context and their own contri- bution to it. For who would be to say that young men and women trained in theology would not in the long run make better administra- tors or leaders than graduates in political economy or administration?

That somewhat extreme and perhaps fanciful illustration of academic freedom was deliberately chosen to exemplify the other end of the continuum from the absolute State control of the curriculum to be observed in China. The reality is much nearer the centre, certainly in the West and, I suspect, in not a few socialist countries as well. What is now interesting in international comparisons is to what extent and in what ways the State will call the tune, what will be the new limits to autonomy. As we have seen, a cardinal issue will be the question of relevance. For politicians who wish to pursue it there is for example excellent copy to be derived from the old pastime of reading through the titles of theses and research projects. Thus Mr Jo Grimond, Chancellor of the University of Kent, in his address at the recent graduation ceremony revealed that "no less than three universities in different continents have been jointly examining the domestic cats of Shetland" and that he knew of a trust which had "received a well-supported plea to finance a study of social deprivation in left-handed immigrants". It makes a nice joke but like many good jokes it is as disturbing as it is funny.

So much, for the moment, for the question of relevance. In order to survey the other argument, the democratic one, and to see some of the practical consequences that derive from it we must ironically turn away from the socialist States where expansion has generally to be reconciled with identifiable economic requirements. Instead, we must look to the United States to see the effects of meeting the increasing appetite for knowledge exhibited by a mass democracy. First we should recall the multiversity idea set out by Clark Kerr in the Godkin Lectures at Harvard in 1963. By subsuming all the disparate elements in higher education, all the purveyors of its infinite variety, the university could become a multiversity and fulfil a duty to serve the whole of civilization. Everyone would have the right to share membership of the same community, one from which inhibiting value judgements attaching to traditional status and prestige had disappeared. Here was an egalitarian vision for those who declared that higher education had an obligation to meet the demands of a mass democracy.

Now that numerical pressures have caused the multiversity idea to be taken seriously in Western Europe, as for example in the German proposals for *Gesamthochschulen*, it is particularly timely to survey the evidence of the Carnegie Commission, the most extensive investigation of the higher education system ever undertaken in the United States. Though in favour of increased equality of opportunity, it predicted the end of the acceleration in the enrolment rate of the post-war period. It suggested in fact that the danger is that the expansion which *has* taken place has already outstripped potential demand so that as a result "the competition for students . . . in the 1980s may lead some institutions to lower their academic standards and even to have no standards at all".

Again and again the Commission's final report returns to questions of quality, intellectual standards and scope for fundamental research that is not excessively constrained by the need for early and obvious practical pay-off. Its express advice is that

"elite institutions of all types—colleges and universities—should be protected and encouraged as a source of scholarship and leadership training at the highest levels. They should not be homogenized in the name of egalitarianism".

So in the Commission's view the realization of equality of opportunity is unlikely to come through bigger and bigger universities, through what it calls universal attendance. To advance social justice it advocates much greater emphasis on alternatives to university. But even though the idea of universal attendance at university is no longer seriously entertained, there would seem to be no going back on the stage of open access after completion of high school and this still represents an advance a good way beyond anything yet experienced in the United Kingdom. Just as China was an extreme case which illuminated the problems associated with relevance, so the United States is in British eyes an extreme example that throws into relief the dilemmas that accompany democratization on a massive scale. And even at this extreme the Carnegie analysis would appear to suggest above all that university and post-secondary education are unlikely to become synonymous terms; that at some point there has to be a differentiation of functions and therefore that tertiary education will continue to comprise a non-university as well as a university sector.

Having looked to East and West let me now summarize the problems involved in meeting the two main criticisms we have been considering. First, the question of relevance. It may well be that much of what is studied in universities *has* become too remote from the realities of national life and that the forces of inertia can too easily prevent change. But, to reiterate, when the cry for relevance is raised, the vital question is who should be the arbiter of what is relevant. Eastern Europe and China have provided ready illustrations of how that relevance can be determined exclusively in accordance with the political and ideological theories and convictions of a national government, how research and teaching can be made subservient to a unitary conception of how society is to be ordered. However outlandish such procedures may seem to us it would be idle to ignore that governments in the West are also tempted to exercise a measure of direction of this kind. Ultimately it is a matter of the balance struck between independence and control.

Now as was pointed out earlier there is a growing number of ways in which the universities and other institutions are financially be-holden to the State and we cannot point to any shiningly inviolable principle of academic independence; if we could, there would be no such phenomenon as the University College at Buckingham. But nor, one hopes, is total political control really conceivable. Sir Kenneth Berrill, in his address to the European Rectors a week or two ago, identified four areas in which there might legitimately be scope for autonomy in the universities: first, the freedom for them to undertake the kind of research they wish, provided they can get it funded, and to disseminate its results; second, room for manoeuvre in determining the content of courses; third, the right to select students where selection is part of the system, provided that the methods are openly determined and conducted; fourth, freedom in the appointment of staff, particularly at the more junior levels (*The Times Higher Educational Supplement*, 1974). And so the field broadens out when considerations of relevance lead on to the question of autonomy.

What is of practical interest is that between the two hypothetical extremes of total independence on the one hand and total political control on the other, there is a no-man's-land of multidimensional debate, conflict and decision, embracing all four fields that Sir Kenneth outlined, coloured by the issue of who has the right to formulate the principles that are to be followed, and reflecting throughout the fluctuating influence of individuals and groups. Autonomous research bodies may resist control of their budgets and direction of their activities by governments: with or without success. Junior staff or students may press for the introduction of a new interdisciplinary syllabus: with or without success. Innovative external examiners at Advanced level may try to change the emphasis among the skills that are valued in potential university entrants: with or without success. These are only a few of countless examples of the course that educational development follows in a pluralistic system. Some of the outcomes are more important than others. Not all of them are at all obviously related to one another. But when assembled, these various developments form the mosaic which is the face of higher education as we know it. And in the United Kingdom at any rate this face has over the years been pretty acceptable. It is still very largely a matter for academics themselves to decide what relevance their activity should have to the national interest, to determine into what sort of hideously relevant scowl this hitherto acceptable face should be distorted.

The second specific question is whether wholesale democratization would bring about distortion to the point of unrecognizability. The areas enumerated by Sir Kenneth Berrill can be drawn together under this theme too. What would be the consequences if we were to dismiss the warnings of the Carnegie Commission as the rearguard action of a handful of senior academics who just want to stop the boat rocking? Here I think it is valuable and instructive to examine what has been happening in the rest of Western Europe, particularly France and the Federal Republic of Germany, two countries much further along the road to democratization than we in the United Kingdom are.

In the background loom the famous "events" of 1968. France in fact provides a telling example of how institutions of higher education can capsize in the inundation of enrolments that results from rapid expansion at the secondary school level. In 1957 the number of pupils who passed the *baccalaureat* was 48,982; in 1967 it was 133,257. As a result of this the French higher education system was precipitated into an open access situation approaching that which has long obtained in the United States. The reason was that the *baccalaureat* had always discharged two functions simultaneously, that of a leaving certificate in the sense of a record of achievement and that of an examination to qualify for university entrance. It is difficult for the British to understand the aura that, until recently anyway, attached to the *baccalaureat*. It was discussed with a reverence that bordered on the religious, it could compete with the Tour de France in the impact it made on French life. Most important, few of those who passed it declined to exercise the automatic right which it gave them to enrol in the university faculty of their choice. And though in the 1960s there were many trivial motives for continuing formal education in this way, at bottom few of those who did so doubted that by enrolling in a faculty they were stepping on to an escalator that would convey them serenely to the world of professional prestige and security.

Much the same is true of the Federal Republic of Germany though the explosion of numbers there came rather later than in France. In fact it was very largely alarmist reaction to the French expansion that prompted the Germans to follow the same course. Georg Picht's notorious and vastly influential publication *The German Educational Catastrophe* had this to say in 1964 about the *Abiturienten*, the German counterparts of the French *bacheliers*:

> "The number of *Abiturienten* is a gauge of the intellectual potential of a nation . . . For the remainder of the twentieth century the balance of interest in Europe will be determined by the fact that, despite a smaller population, France will for an indefinite period of years produce almost

three times as many *Abiturienten* as the Federal Republic . . . the French sociologist Alfred Sauvy bases on this the convincing forecast that France will be the centre of Europe in 1970". (Picht, 1964.)

The *Abitur* is very comparable to the *baccalaureat* in terms of prestige and in the rights it confers. And by virtue of its strong element of internal assessment it is even less capable of being manipulated as a selective mechanism. So Germany too has had to act in the face of sudden open access conditions.

When the responses to the resulting malaise are surveyed, the French measures show up in a spectacular light. A characteristically precise analysis of the problems led to the *loi d'orientation* which meant nothing less than the removal of the university system set up by Napoleon 150 years earlier and its replacement by something entirely new. The old faculties were dissolved and replaced by smaller units called *unites d'enseignement et de recherche*. These new small universities were to have a substantial measure of autonomy, to be interdisciplinary in character and their reduced size combined with their emancipation from the central control of the old Napeolonic system were considered the preconditions for a less impersonal atmosphere in which better relations between staff and students could be fostered.

Of the three key words which characterise the new law—*participation, multidisciplinarité, autonomie*—participation appeared in the short run the most compelling issue. In the longer run however the other two have been more significant. The logic behind the multidisciplinary idea was that if the work of the old subject centred faculties was appropriate for only that fraction of students who could expect to find employment in the learned professions, particularly university and *lycee* teaching, as was patently the case, then clearly for the others new courses had to be developed that would make sense in more generally vocational terms. Those other walks of life that would eventually absorb graduates required a rather more versatile and practical product than the university lecturer or school-master manqué. But what in fact appears to have been happening is that the new smaller universities have to a very large extent been able to organize their work on a single subject basis as before. It would seem that the cases where the new organizational structure has actually been accompanied by a reorganization of curricula have been few and far between.

Another provision of the *loi d'orientation* was even more significant; this was the article which gave universities the power to introduce a probation period for new entrants. There had been no question of denying admission to those who had gained the *baccalaureat*, but it was possible to use the assessments at the end of the probation period as a way of cutting down drastically on numbers—it was not unusual for these to be halved after the first year. In short the granting of autonomy to the new universities had the effect of handing the initiative to the university teachers in the two important spheres of who and what they would teach. The result has been to put a sharp brake on the advance towards a universal access situation which had been brought about by the huge increase in numbers acquiring the *baccalaureat*. The collective behaviour of the academic profession has been to use its newly won powers not to embrace expansion but to combat it. While the law is a good example of the French inclination to scrap existing institutions and start again from scratch, it also calls to mind that peculiarly French proverb *Plus çà change, plus c'est la même chose*. Perhaps the most telling illustration of the uninterrupted adherence to elitist ideas in France is the fact that throughout the convulsions of the past decade the super-elite *grandes ecoles* have remained unscathed.

Turning from France to the Federal Republic of Germany we find similar measures being taken to cope with the expansion, with some *Lander* dissolving the old faculties and substituting structures designed to promote interdisciplinary courses appropriate to the needs of the enlarged clientele—the argument about relevance again. But there is one crucial difference. In contrast to the central control of the Napoleonic system the German universities had from the time of Humboldt embodied ideas of academic freedom and autonomy. The accusation directed at them in the last decade has been that they have defaulted on the unwritten obligations that accompany these privileges, above all the obligation to take account of the welfare of students and junior academic staff.

So the business of making changes to cope with expansion has turned, not on the increasing of autonomy as in France but on its curtailment. The legislation that is currently under consideration, the higher education law or *Hochschulrahmengesetz*, is designed to provide a framework within which the existing institutions of higher education can be merged into large comprehensive universities. For clearly the creation of comprehensive universities provides a plausible political response to the social pressure for democratization and the economic pressure for more relevant curricula. We are back to the multiversity of Clark Kerr.

In so far as the process of reorganization is already under way, what makes the German situation similar to that in France is the manifest reluctance to play the interdisciplinary game, a reluctance that does not appear to have diminished with the reorganization into teaching departments. Indeed in the case of the comprehensive University of Kassel which has been hailed in some quarters as a prototype, there has been an additional reorganization into "learning departments". Thus there is one departmental structure arranging the courses being offered and a quite separate one arranging what items the students will choose from the *à la carte* menu which these courses constitute (*Frankfurter Allgemeine Zeitung*, 1974). The potential for polarization is obvious whether one sees it as between research and teaching or between two different views of the nature of teaching in a university. A good focus for the conflict can generally be found in the attitudes to the building up of the central university library, the keystone of traditional academic research and consequently a prime target for those who wish to diminish this feature of university activity.

What is interesting about these developments is the emergence of an article of political faith to the effect that a reorientation of the attitudes, aims and methods of university teachers can be brought about by changing the institutions. Now this is a hypothesis that deserves scrutiny. The kind of attitudes I am referring to are contained in the cluster identified by Halsey and Trow in their study, *The British Academics* (1971), attitudes which can broadly be described as conventionally academic, characterized by the concern to guarantee conditions in which research can function, in which teaching can be in depth and grow out of this research, the concern to be correspondingly selective about who should enjoy the benefits of this level of teaching, and to ensure that new entrants to the teaching community accept its established criteria—publication of research in reputable journals, for example—in short, broadly share the established view of how the university world should operate. The fact that this conservative position is fairly characteristic of British university teachers as a group does not suggest an auspicious outlook for any reorganization along mass higher education lines that might take place in the United Kingdom. Furthermore, the evidence from France in recent years, though admittedly not very systematically collected and documented as yet; is more apposite still, for it suggests that amid the turmoil of reorganization that has been taking place there, a similar cluster of traditionally academic attitudes is successfully reasserting itself. And it reappears in the report on the Carnegie Commission.

I would contend that a similarly oriented group could be identified in Germany. It has long been the case that the homogeneity of the university sector there has been in accordance with the lead given in setting standards by different universities in different fields, by a kind of Ivy League of faculties or departments. The real point about the creation of *Gesamthochschulen* is that the homogeneity of the academic community that has been familiar in the past will be removed and that two quite different conceptions of the task of the university will take root. The further assumption is that under the new dispensation, what we might call the conventionally academic group, retaining something of the Humboldt inspiration, will in turn find a new orientation, falling in with the majority view in these greatly expanded and ostentatiously democratic institutions—although none of the evidence we have surveyed suggests that this is likely.

Yet there is in Germany a good deal of new wisdom to the effect that the old model is being superseded inexorably by a new one which is in tune with the conditions of mass industrial democracy, that Humboldt's principles have gone for good, that the era of the *Gesamtho-chschule* is here to stay and that eventually the rest of us will follow suit. Now no other Western European country has embarked upon this kind of violation of the security of academic men to such a potentially extreme degree. It can however be presented in quite plausible terms. After all, is it not merely putting to the test at the level of higher education a process that has in recent decades been familiar in the domain of secondary education. There have been plenty of examples of how comprehensive school systems have been introduced in the teeth of the opposition of the more academically oriented teachers. But the conventional wisdom has been that while these teachers may bleat about having to change their whole approach to their work in the face of the new tasks and conditions imposed upon them and the new problems they have to solve—to be tolerant rather than rigorous, child-centred rather than subject-centred and so on—while they may bleat about this, they always come round and accept in the end. What the *Gymnasium* teachers have begun to face in the context of the comprehensive school, the *Gesamtschule*, lies just around the corner for their university colleagues in the context of the comprehensive university, the *Gesamthochschule*.

Well, are the university teachers going to come round in the end and what are the pressures that will be exerted to force them to do so? In practical terms it is going to boil down to how far politico-administrative decisions regarding financial provision, open admission, teaching loads and appointment of staff will be able to hamper or even to destroy the conditions in which research and higher level teaching can flourish. This struggle is not straightforwardly between politicians and academics, not just between governments and universities, for with the creation of *Gesamthochschulen* there has ceased to be a unitary conception of what a university should be. Rather it will be fought out between warring factions within institutions, whether they go by the name of teaching departments and learning departments or something else.

What is building up in Germany is something of an Armageddon between those concerned to defend the traditional freedoms and those who are following the political urge to make a great show of coming to terms with the new social and economic forces which I mentioned at the beginning. It is no doubt true that the ferocity of the struggle can be attributed to the abuses of these freedoms that were evident in the past: to some degree autocratic professors of yesterday have reaped the whirlwind of today. Perhaps the saddest omission after the war was the failure to take the kind of action urged by our own AUT delegation which visited the country during the Occupation period. Be the reasons as they may, the battle is being joined and it is one which is relevant for all Western European countries.

It seems to me likely that there will be no unilateral victory but that the forces of traditional scholarship or reactionary elitism, depending on your point of view, will regroup on a more specifically institutional basis than before, and that the Ivy League of faculties or departments will give way to an Ivy League of specific institutions where these forces will be strong enough to maintain their own standards. I would guess further that most *Land* governments will be prepared to accept this development as long as the institutions concerned earn their keep by virtue of their academic achievements, the quality of their research and teaching. It will mean a *de facto* binary system of a much less acceptable kind than the one in the United Kingdom for it will be based on a difference in quality and status rather than a difference in function. The elite group is as likely to include technological universities or higher vocational institutions as it is universities which are centres of more traditional scholarship.

Let me conclude by submitting to you that we should be very suspicious of the seductive theory that all-embracing tertiary education agglomerates would rid us of the differences of status and prestige that cause irritation and resentment. It is preferable to be saddled with such superficial irritants in their present form rather than to place in jeopardy what in my view really matters, namely the conditions under which research and teaching at the highest levels can flourish. If this suggests an aversion to challenge, playing safe by sticking with the established differentiations within higher education, so be it.

This paper has the rather pedestrian title "International Differences in Higher Education"; if I were to give it spice with a more incisive sub-title it would be "Learning to Live with Elites".

## References

*Frankfurter Allgemeine Zeitung.* (1974). 7 August.

Halsey, A. H. and Trow, H. (1971). *The British Academics.* London: Faber & Faber.

*The Irish Times.* (1974). 2 January.

*The Observer.* (1973). 30 December.

Picht, G. (1964). *Die Deutsche Bildungskatstrophe.* Olten/Freiburg im Breisgau: Walter-Verlag.

*The Times Higher Educational Supplement.* (1974). 7 August.

*World Yearbook of Education for 1971/72.* (1971). London: Evans Brothers.

# Student Participation and Higher Education

## J. T. PARK

*Department of Adult Education and Extramural Studies,*
*University of Leeds, Leeds, England*

My contribution will be personal rather than statistical because what I have to say will be drawn largely from my own experience, both as a teacher and as a Member of Parliament during which time I was a member of the House of Commons Select Committee on Education. It will also, in a sense, be prejudiced, but I hope that it will be the prejudice of experience rather than of dogma.

A large part of my professional life has been spent in a sector of education in which student participation has not just been a desirable objective but a basic necessity. The adult education sector, as we have known it in this country, could never have existed in its traditional form had it not been founded on principles involving student participation.

The students who come to WEA or extramural classes are volunteers and not conscripts. They do not come because it is necessary for them to obtain specific professional qualifications; they come because they are interested. They stay because they become involved; they benefit because they feel that they have participated in an educational process. Voting with the feet is an effective expression of opinion in any context, and voting with the feet in adult education classes results in the collapse of the classes. Therefore, in order to preserve classes it is necessary for tutors and organizing institutions to bear in mind student wishes and to plan teaching approaches and syllabuses in the light of student demands. The students' studies must be seen by them, and not merely by their teachers, as being relevant to their needs. This implies a share on the part of the student, both in planning of programmes and in their pedagogical treatment.

Education is recognized in the adult sector as being a group experience not a one-way communication. The teacher's role is recognized as being to make the group experience an effective one so that all—including the tutor—can learn from each other. The education of the individual, or of the group, must be seen in some way to relate to the requirements of society as a whole—not necessarily to its social or political requirements. This is because adult education is a form of education for social responsibility perhaps in a more direct sense than other aspects of education. I believe that this form of education is a form of student participation. Before I became a Member of Parliament, and before I served on the Select Committee, if I had been asked to define what was meant by student participation I think I would have defined it in these terms—in the terms of the adult educational concept and in terms of the education process rather than in terms of educational institutions.

The second strand of personal experience which is relevant to my contribution, comes from my membership of the Parliamentary Select Committee and, in particular, from its investigations into students and their relations with universities and colleges, which took place during the Parliamentary Session of 1968 to 1969 (House of Commons Select Committee on Education and Science, 1973). That Committee did not feel it sufficient to take evidence at Westminster from representatives of students, academic staffs, administrative staff, vice-chancellors, etc. It was also concerned to go out into the field, to visit colleges and universities and to find how closely the actual experience of university life and relationships related to the rather theoretical concepts which were sometimes presented to us by all sides when we held our hearings in Westminster.

I soon found that the definitions of student participation which were current in the universities and colleges were very different from the adult educational concepts of student participation—to which I have referred. There were at least three different approaches to the subject of student participation which could be discerned and these different approaches often contradicted each other.

For example, there was what might be called the "constitutional" approach. The participation was to be measured by the number of seats which student representatives held on faculty boards, senates, university councils or college governing bodies. The views about the desirable number would, of course, vary greatly depending on whether we were talking to vice-chancellors and principals or to representatives of students. Nevertheless, the constitutionalist view seemed to me to be derived from a rather simplistic belief that committees really did make decisions, and that representation on committees would make a basic difference to the methods of policy determination within the institutions. It seemed that those who held the constitutionalist view and who argued that there should be student participation on these committees, were concerning themselves much more with education structure than with the process of education, and with a concept of participation which was in many ways far from complete.

The second approach could be described as the "revolutionary" view of student participation—a view which found no support at all amongst administrators and very little amongst university or college teachers. However, it was a view which was held sincerely by a significant number of student representatives who gave evidence to us. They believed that institutions of higher education were in reality little more than battlefields in the class war. They took the view that administrative and higher academic staffs were in the position of rulers, whilst students and junior staff were in the position of a repressed proletariat. Their objective in seeking participation was not merely to secure representation on committees; their objective was to provoke confrontation in order to win power and yet, at the same time as taking this view, they recognized that their fight for power could never really be successful within the existing social system anyway. It is a point of view which is expressed fairly graphically by Anthony Arblaster (1974) in his recent book on academic freedom, in which he writes that

"In the last analysis an education free from authoritarianism and free from the distortions currently imposed upon it by capitalism and the capitalist state, cannot exist within the context of capitalism and authoritarianism in society as a whole. That is why the fight for freedom and democracy in education must also be a struggle for revolutionary social change."

—certainly a very different concept of participation from the adult education model which was described earlier.

Finally, there is what might be called the "trade union" view of participation. It falls somewhere between the constitutional and revolutionary conceptions, and is more often an implicit view than an explicit one. It shares with the constitutional view a belief in the importance of student membership of representative institutions; it shares with the revolutionary view a denial that such membership and representation can ever in itself produce a complete community of interest between students, staff and administrators. It differs from the constitutional view in regarding representation as a means to an end rather than an end in itself, but it differs from the revolutionary view in regarding the end to be achieved as not a final, great confrontation but rather some form of continual balance between contending parties.

I have now defined at least four different conceptions of the meaning of student participation. I have done so because I believe that there is very often a great deal of confusion as to which definition any particular protagonist is maintaining at any one time. Given the definitions, we must now attempt some evaluation of their usefulness as guides to understanding the problem.

I return to the adult educational concept, the least controversial of the four, the most easily accepted because of its imprecision, the one which everybody can interpret to suit himself—whether he be an educational authoritarian or an educational anarchist—and one which is often stated in such extremely general terms that it rarely receives the serious attention which it warrants.

Nevertheless, the adult educational concept of student participation raises a few quite serious questions. First, how far can a theory which, in essence, is a distillation of the practical experience of one sector of education be readily transferred to another? Is it, in fact, possible to adopt towards a sixteen- to eighteen-year-old student the same kind of teaching approach which is usually adopted for mature students in adult education classes? To what extent are those without personal experience of life, and those whose social awareness is perhaps not yet fully developed, capable of benefiting from a form of participation which assumes that all those who are taking part have reached a certain level of understanding and responsibility? At the very least the question poses problems. Secondly, how far is this method of participation adaptable to subjects outside the social sciences where the process of formal, factual learning is more important and analyses of conflicting theories and interpretations much less so?

Thirdly, if one accepts that the adult educational concept of participation ought to be spread through other sectors, how is this to be brought about when so much depends upon individual teachers, students and classes? These are questions which I raise, not as objections to the theory but rather as difficulties which are to be encountered if one attempts to transfer to one sector of education a concept of participation which is rooted in the experience of another.

The attempts which have been made recently within the universities to broaden curricula, to develop interdisciplinary courses, to encourage the growth of team planning and teaching and so on, have in some cases been far from completely successful. Mr Eric Hewton in a recent article in *The Times Higher Educational Supplement* (1974) showed how tenuous some of these experiments have been. At the end of his article he expressed the view that they were very far from being established as the norm, and that indeed there were possibilities on the part of university teachers of a movement to a return to a greater specialization and a greater traditionalism.

I move next to the constitutionalist position, to a view which I described as maintaining that student participation is to be measured in terms of the number of seats which students hold on committees. There are a number of serious criticisms which can be made against this view. If it is being argued seriously that by putting student representatives on committees, a community of interests is being created, and what is essentially a problem of communications is being solved, this is a short-sighted view and one which completely overlooks the fact that there are genuine and real conflicts of interest between educational participants, between teachers and students, between administrators and academic staffs, between—if you like—all the other people also employed in universities.

Electing people to committees in no way succeeds in abolishing interest conflicts. It may, under certain circumstances, sharpen them. The second criticism of this view is that it assumes that committees in fact make decisions. Those who are associated with university and college government are well aware that committees much more often only legitimize decisions which have been made elsewhere. Indeed, in the case of many universities where there is a great complexity of committees, it is often almost impossible to disentangle where the process of decision making starts and where it finishes. Very often the vital elements of the process do not take place within formal committees, but in much more informal ways in between committee meetings. It is interesting to note that student representatives who, a few years ago, were the most enthusiastic advocates of the idea of representational committees are now themselves beginning to question seriously whether such participation is in itself what they seek to obtain. Indeed, they are beginning to ask whether committee representation is worthwhile at all, unless accompanied by more fundamental change.

Next, the revolutionary approach. The main weakness about this is that it is not really about education at all, but political ideology. The idea of participation is here used as a weapon in the ideological struggle, and is not intended as a method of reforming university and college administration but as a method of changing the fundamental basis of society. I am not saying that it is wrong to change the fundamental basis of society; it may in fact be the right thing to do, but that is not a subject which there is time to explore here. It is however pertinent to note that for those who are concerned to change the fundamental basis of society there would seem to be far more sensitive points at which to operate than the university campus. Those who are concerned to make this change will not do so by occupying the lecture hall at the London School of Economics or the vice-chancellor's office at the University of Essex. In a way, such activities far from being parts of a real battle are a diversion from it, and they may well create a situation in which, instead of society being changed, the organizations which want to preserve it as it is become greatly strengthened.

Of course, there is a much more conventional criticism of the revolutionary view: if the aim is confrontation and a continued series of crises, how far is that aim compatible with the existence of institutions of higher learning at all, how far is it possible to carry out an educational process when the brickbats, and perhaps worse, are flying around the whole of the time? This argument also is not without some merit.

I come now to the trade union view, which in some ways, seems to be an extremely powerful one. It recognizes that there is a conflict of interest and that there will continue to be tensions and differences, but it also believes that such conflicts and tensions can in fact lead to creative solutions rather than to confrontations. It accepts that a situation of balance will continue. This view too is open to some criticism. The analogy between industry and education is not a very accurate one. Students are not wage-earners, professors and lecturers are not employers or foremen, the maximization of profit is not the objective of an educational institution, and the process of learning is very different from the process of production.

Thus, all of these views are open to serious criticism. All of them may contain some elements which are useful. But if any of them is based on the idea that participation will eliminate tension then it is based on a false premise. The whole process of education itself is one which inevitably involves tension, a tension which gives life to the whole concept of higher and further education. What we must seek to do is to try to find means of ensuring that the tension is creative rather than destructive; representation on committees may have a part to play in this but no more important a part than the adult educational concept of participation in the process of education as opposed to the institutional framework. The theory of structural democracy—which the advocates of representation on committees put forward—is not in itself complete. We need to think in terms not simply of defining what we mean by participation, but also in terms of what we mean by education. If we think in both of these ways then we will probably find that one cannot really exist without the other. They are in fact different but complementary aspects of an identical basic process.

## References

Arblaster, A. (1974). *Academic Freedom*. London: Penguin Books.

House of Commons Select Committee on Education and Science. (1973). *Student Relations: Report and Minutes of Evidence*. London: HMSO.

Hewton, E. (1974). Consumer concern as a teaching principle. *The Times Higher Education Supplement*. 23 August 1974.

# Aims of Today in the Education of the Lawyer

## S. B. MARSH

*Department of Law, Manchester Polytechnic, Manchester, England*

## The Problems

In 1450, at the time of the peasants' revolt, if Shakespeare is to be believed, Dick the Butcher said to Jack Cade, "The first thing we do, let's kill all the lawyers". If this proposal had been accepted and put into effect, we might have been spared many of the problems facing legal education today.

The education and training of lawyers in England and Wales is complicated by the fact that there are two branches of the legal profession, a small practising Bar with some 3,000 members and the much larger solicitors' branch with now about 30,000 practitioners. Whilst much of the training is common for both barristers and solicitors, there are important differences in the knowledge and skills necessary for success in each branch of the profession and these must be reflected in the training. In addition, the Bar has for many years assumed the burden of training lawyers for practice in Commonwealth countries, although the number of these students has fallen considerably in recent years with the establishment of overseas law schools.

Perhaps a more important problem arises from the relatively small part that has been played by the universities in the education of professional lawyers. In most other countries, including Scotland, the law taught in the universities and the law practised in the courts was the same, and from earliest times a close relationship was established between academics and practitioners. In this country, the universities, in particular Oxford and Cambridge, were concerned originally with the study of Civil or Roman Law. On the other hand, the local law was the English common law and, to meet the needs of practice, the profession set up its own law schools to teach the common law to would-

117

be practitioners. By the time that the teaching of English law had become widespread throughout our universities, the professional law schools had become well-established, and this dual system of law teaching has continued down to the present day. Among the results of this historical development are the failure of the legal profession to make full use of our public education system and the mistrust and suspicion which still persists between academics and practitioners.

The growth of university law teaching has not been entirely ignored by the profession. From 1922 onwards, certain limited exemptions from the professional examinations have been given to law graduates on a subject by subject basis and graduate articled clerks have been granted a reduction in the period of articles. Also in 1922, the Law Society, recognizing the value of a period of full-time study in an academic institution, introduced the compulsory academic year for all articled clerks other than law graduates which was mainly undertaken at provincial universities. These additional students and the financial subsidy paid by the Law Society became less important to the universities after the war and the system was discontinued in 1962. It was then intended that all tuition would be concentrated in the Law Society's own College of Law but the pressure of numbers led to the recognition of professional law courses in seven colleges of commerce, now polytechnics.

Apart from this limited recognition of university law teaching, the professional training of lawyers has been carried out by the profession. Almost from time immemorial this training has been based upon a form of apprenticeship, pupillage for barristers and articles for solicitors. This apprenticeship has been supported by a system of qualifying examinations for which tuition has largely been provided by the professional law schools. Until recently, entry into the profession has tended to be restricted to those who could obtain parental or other support during the period of apprenticeship and for the period after qualification until they had built up a successful practice.

The social changes which followed the second World War have had important consequences for the profession. The great expansion of higher education and the connected extension of student grants has led to a great increase in the number of law students and much wider sources of recruitment to the profession. The Law has also been obliged to recognize, albeit slowly, that young people can command higher rates of pay at an earlier age in other occupations, that they often wish to marry earlier, and that they are reluctant to be dependent upon their parents for financial support, even if their parents are able to provide this support.

The traditional legal apprenticeship, particularly articles, has therefore come under some strain. The apprentice has sought to earn a living whilst learning. The master has been reluctant both to pay and to instruct; he has expected profitable work from his articled clerk because of the shorter period of articles and because his previous legal education gives him a greater economic value. At the same time, the considerable variation which has always existed in the efficiency of the instruction between one master and another has become more obvious in our modern society. Grave doubts have been expressed as to the continuing viability of a system of articles which has led to much debate and discussion over the past few years.

## The Ormrod Report

In December 1967, the Lord Chancellor appointed a Committee under the Chairmanship of Mr Justice Ormrod to consider and make recommendations upon training for the legal profession. This was the first exhaustive examination of legal education since that carried out by a Select Committee of the House of Commons in 1846. A substantial body of evidence, both written and oral, was received and considered over a period of three years and the Committee's Report was published in March 1971 (Committee on Legal Education, 1971).

The Ormrod Report defined the fundamental problem as that of combining the education which is necessary to enable a person to follow a "learned" profession with instruction in the skills and techniques which are essential to its actual practice. Whilst experience in practice is essential, the best use should be made of the facilities available in institutions of higher education following the great expansion of university and polytechnic law schools. This should then be supplemented by training in professional skills and techniques.

The Report stressed the need to integrate academic education and professional training as in the medical profession. It recommended the acceptance of the law degree as a major part of the professional qualification. In this way, and with the assistance of some change in attitudes, the traditional gulf between the academics and the practitioners could be bridged with great benefit to the profession. The duplication between the public and professional law schools would be removed and scarce resources in the form of accommodation, library provision and teaching staff would be saved.

It was therefore recommended that the education and training of the professional lawyer required three stages: first, the academic stage to be carried out in a university or polytechnic: secondly, the professional stage consisting partly of institutional training and partly of practical experience; thirdly, provision should be made for continuing education or training after qualification.

## THE ACADEMIC STAGE

The Ormrod Committee felt that the academic stage should provide the student with three of the essential requirements of the practitioner, a basic knowledge of the law and where to find it, an understanding of the relationship of law to the social and economic environment in which it operates, and the ability to handle facts and to apply abstract concepts to those facts. The student accordingly needs specific training in law, but this should be broadly based with some exposure to other disciplines. At the same time, he must develop the intellectual processes which are usually referred to as "thinking like a lawyer".

After considerable discussion the Committee was unanimous that these objects would be best attained by reading for a law degree. Whilst there are examples of successful lawyers who have read another subject at university, the extra time then needed to acquire the basic legal knowledge, perhaps without the help of a grant, would raise too many difficulties for most students. We are concerned with training the average practitioner, not the future Lord Chancellor. The law degree was therefore to be the normal, though not the exclusive, way into the profession and it was expected that this would cover some 90% of entrants.

An alternative method of entry was proposed for those people without law degrees who might wish to join the profession and who had other qualities which made them desirable entrances. This was to be the common professional examination, so called because it would be common to both Bar and Law Society students. It would normally require two years' preparation and would be open to certain restricted classes of students; graduates in other disciplines, mature students who had qualifications or experience in other fields, and legal executives who had worked in the law in an unqualified capacity. It would not be open to school leavers.

Insistence upon a largely graduate entry would have little effect upon the Bar with its small number of students of whom the majority are already graduates. It would affect considerably the Law Society with much larger student numbers of whom only about 50% are graduates. It would require a considerable expansion of law degree places at universities and polytechnics. Statistics are not easily available but it would appear that two-thirds of all law graduates enter the profession. Thus three extra law degree places must be provided to obtain two professional lawyers.

## THE PROFESSIONAL STAGE

After completing the academic stage either by law degree or common professional examination, the student would pass on to the professional stage. This would cover the period until he is permitted to engage in practice on his own account. The aims of this stage would be to enable the student to adapt his academic knowledge to the conditions of practice and to acquire the necessary professional techniques and expertise.

The Ormrod Committee's view was that, whilst good articles and good pupillage provided excellent professional training, the present system left too much to chance. Too much depended upon the conscientiousness and competence of the principal or pupil-master and the nature of his practice. If he is busy, he will have little time for instruction. If he is not busy, he will not be able to give his articled clerks or pupils the instruction they need. It was felt that much of the knowledge and experience, at present acquired by apprenticeship could be imparted more efficiently by a systematic course of vocational training in an institutional environment.

It was therefore recommended that all students should first take a full-time vocational course of one-year's duration. The course would include some additional law subjects of a more directly practical application, some non-law subjects of special concern to practitioners—elementary behavioural science and business finance were suggested as examples—and, perhaps of greatest importance, a series of practical exercises. The object of these exercises would be training not by telling or showing but by doing. Students would be presented with simulated real life situations and act for one of the parties involved, drafting letters and documents and carrying through the necessary negotiations. Thus the conveyance of a piece of property, the administration of a deceased person's estate or the formation of a company would be taken through all the stages in a comparatively short period of time. Under the present apprenticeship system such a complete picture of a legal transaction is rarely obtained.

The second part of the professional stage would be a period of practical experience or in-training. In the case of barristers this would be twelve months' pupillage, since the Bar is organized on an individual basis and there appears to be no practical alternative. With the advantage of the vocational year, the pupillage should be more meaningful than at present. Solicitors would be given a limited practising certificate which would prevent them from entering into a partnership or practising on their own account for three years, thus ensuring office training under supervision. As qualified solicitors instead of articled clerks they should be accorded a higher status and a more adequate remuneration than at present. Experience in other countries supports this view.

## CONTINUING EDUCATION

The third stage of the training process—continuing education—was not developed in depth by the Ormrod Committee. It was pointed out that in a rapidly changing world it was not possible to regard the moment of qualification as the high water mark after which no further training was necessary. It was not possible to equip the lawyer at qualification with a comprehensive knowledge of every subject he may encounter in practice, and education and training must be a continuous process through a lawyer's professional life.

A considerable amount of work is already taking place in this field. Interest in research into various aspects of the working of the law is expanding and many courses and conferences are offered by a number of bodies. The Committee felt that this area offered the largest prospects of growth in the training of practising lawyers and recommended a need for organization and stimulation. An Institute of Professional Legal Studies was suggested. No positive action of this nature, however, has since been taken.

## The Reception of Ormrod

### THE ACADEMIC STAGE

In general, the Ormrod proposals for the academic stage have been largely accepted. Both branches of the profession are working towards a largely law graduate entry and a common professional examination is being planned for the minority in the special categories already mentioned. A large expansion of law degree places is taking place and there is certainly no shortage of applicants for these places. An Advisory Committee on Legal Education has been set up to act as a link between the academic law schools and the profession, and to advise on the recognition of degrees, particularly where law has been read along with some other subject.

The profession is prepared to give up teaching at the academic stage provided that it is satisfied that the law degree is sufficiently comprehensive. It requires the inclusion of six basic or "core" legal subjects, although without the close scrutiny of syllabus content as in the past when exemptions from professional examinations were sought. This is, however, resented by some academics as an interference with an institutions' freedom to determine its own curricula. The problem is perhaps more apparent than real and may well disappear with the passage of time and the growth of confidence and mutual trust between all concerned with legal education.

## THE PROFESSIONAL STAGE

The Ormrod proposals for the professional stage, in particular the vocational course, have provoked the greatest discussion and controversy. The majority of the Committee members were in favour of the course being mounted by universities and polytechnics. The profession has not accepted this and preferred its own professional law schools. The Bar, again with the advantage of small numbers, is developing a vocational course at the Inns of Court School of Law into which its present Bar Finals course will gradually merge. The Law Society for whom the changes will be more radical has encountered difficulties.

The Law Society was planning a "pilot" vocational course at its College of Law for 240 students in 1975. This was to be followed by an extension of the course to all students, probably about 2,000, two or three years later. Finding additional resources in the form of accommodation and teaching staff of the right type to cater for these numbers is difficult enough, but the real problem has been finance. Government assistance has been refused and it is unrealistic to expect students to pay an economic fee of £700 or more. In addition they would need to maintain themselves for a period of 40 weeks or rely upon a local authority discretionary grant. The effect would be to close the profession to all but the wealthy.

A proposal to meet part at least of the cost by a levy upon practising solicitors has not been received with much enthusiasm. Another proposal to offer the course to universities and polytechnics would be more likely to lead to assistance from public funds. Subsidised fees might then be charged and maintenance grants might be easier to obtain, although there is no certainty about this. The Law Society's view is that this would mean giving up most of its control over entry to the profession which it is most reluctant to do.

Earlier this year a consultative document on the vocational course was circulated to all solicitors and discussed at a series of provincial meetings. The result was a large majority in favour of the retention of articles and against the vocational course. The whole question of the professional stage of training is now back in the melting pot. We do not know what will emerge but a combination of the old and the new is likely—a modified Part II examination following a full-time course of study, a modified form of articles, and attendance at a short full-time course of practical exercises.

## The Future

Looking to the future, there is at present no shortage of potential recruits to the legal profession. The number of suitably qualified applicants is far in excess of the number of law degree places available. At the same time there appears to be a shortage of professionally qualified lawyers, although attempts to quantify this are fraught with difficulties. The qualification period is lengthy and changes such as an extension of legal aid or a State insurance scheme for personal injuries could have an important and immediate effect upon the demand for lawyers.

The first part of the training process is now clear, a law degree course with the assistance of a mandatory grant. It enables a young person to defer his decision as to whether to become a barrister or solicitor or to enter some other form of legal career until he or she knows more of what is involved.

The universities and polytechnics are expanding rapidly to meet the demand for places. They are also modifying their degree courses to meet the needs of the present and the future. Law is no longer taught in a vacuum but attempts are made to show how it affects and is affected by political, social and economic considerations. Traditional legal subject barriers are being broken down and new subjects are emerging. Family law and labour law are now well-established. Poverty law, environmental law and European Community law are emerging. Likely changes in professional practice, for instance, an extension of neighbourhood law centre work, are being recognized.

The doubts now attach to the second or professional part of the training process. The Ormrod Report points the way even though practical considerations may prevent its full implementations. If the profession is to recruit the people that it needs to meet the challenge of the future, it must ensure that potential entrants are not debarred by the expense of qualifying or diverted to other professions by more favourable financial prospects during the qualifying period. Time during the qualifying period is a scarce resource and must be used as efficiently as possible. The previous academic studies of the student must be recognised and built upon, not duplicated. The transition from training and learning to practising and earning must be made as easy as possible.

The lawyer has much to contribute to society. If we can solve the problems of legal education, we may even be glad that all the lawyers were not killed five hundred years ago.

## Reference

Report of the Committee on Legal Education (1971). Chairman: Mr Justice Ormrod. London: HMSO Cmnd. 4595.

# The Education of the Professional and of the Manager

## BERNARD BENJAMIN

*Department of Social Science and Humanities,
City University, London, England*

The education of the manager and the professional is a process of inequality. It has to aim not only to implant information but also to develop particular mental processes—of comparative quantification, of analysis, of logical deduction, of the choice of appropriate techniques among those that have been learned. It follows also that the educational system must be selective of those who have these mental abilities to develop.

It must, in order to avoid waste, quickly reject those who are not adaptable to the role requirements of the professional or the manager. This is, first, because a profession has to underwrite the competence of its members and second, because those who are rejected should find other roles more appropriate to their abilities as early in their formative years as possible.

The objective of this paper is to consider both the professional and the manager. The two roles are different and though the same person can occupy them at different times (even within the hour) and though education for one may help performance in the other one person cannot occupy them both at the same time. The distinction between roles though not necessarily between persons is an important one in many respects especially from an ethical point of view and it has important implications for education.

Let us briefly consider these two roles. First, the manager. We live in a world in which economic activity has become very highly organized. There is inevitably intense specialization of labour and formal structures of organization of extensive size and intricacy. The precise form of the organization appropriate to any economic activity derives from the desired objectives of that activity which also bring the organization into being. Central direction is essential if the component groups of the organization are to work efficiently and in co-ordination over a sustained period of time and with limited resources, towards defined objectives. Management as a function is the exercise of the authority and responsibility implied by this direction; as a body it is that group which wields this authority and responsibility. In speaking of central direction it should be understood that management is hierarchically structured but not necessarily intensely concentrated. Management normally descends through many hierarchical levels with different degrees of responsibility and authority. All this is true of the public services as of private corporations. This direction is both tactical and strategic. The manager is concerned with day to day work direction and the internal services of the organization but his major concern is with planning for the future achievement of the objects of the organization in conditions which cannot be wholly foreseen.

The conditions of uncertainty determine the qualities that have to be cultivated and developed in the manager. The process of decision-taking in these conditions is partly informed, partly intuitive. The manager in any one such decision-taking situation has first to consult experience; his own experience and the experience of others in similar situations to the extent that this can be brought to his attention. He then conceives an analysis of strategies from which to make choices. This analysis if formalized to a degree made possible by information ("research and intelligence" is the current popular term) but some part of it is informal and unverbalized. However inadequate the information, or informal the strategic analysis, the manager must make a choice, stick to it, and be accountable for it. The bad manager is not the one who makes mistakes but the one who either refuses to admit the possibility of error or tries to avoid making any choice. This is what we mean when we repeat the aphorism about the man who never having made a mistake has never done anything.

The role of the professional is not to make strategic choices but to present them. He is required to do all those things which help to illuminate the choices and the risks; to analyse the particular problem for which a strategy has to be developed in such a way that the choices are brought into sharp focus; to use his experience and technique to indicate, as far as information and skills permit, the likely consequences of the available options and thus to narrow the area of uncertainty within which the manager takes decisions. At a later stage the professional must also be able to relate the actual out-turn of events to those stages in the decision process which were, for lack of information, intuitive, and thus bring into relief the specific judgements which were wrong. In this way he improves the learning process of the manager.

The two roles of manager and professional differ in another extremely important respect; one which is the whole basis of professionalism in the very best sense of the term. The manager is entirely committed. He has objectives which he wants to achieve. His decision-making process is constrained only by the extent of his knowledge and the power of his intuition. It is overshadowed by many other factors; personal ambition, the drive toward economic security, preference for particular ideas, loyalties to groups, relationships with colleagues. All these factors exert pressures and may also cloud and confuse issues.

It is vital that information provided by the professional is not affected by pressures of this kind but peculiar to the professional. The manager has got to be able to rely on the complete impartiality and objectivity of the professional so that as far as possible the analysis of the information content of the decision-making process is free of external pressures and related only to the objectives of the organization which the manager is directing. There is much more in this than simply increasing rationality and thereby reducing the frequency of erroneous decisions. There is something called "the public interest". Here we turn to a wider concept of the role of the professional in society. In contrasting the role of the professional and the manager it must not be overlooked that the manager is not the only person who buys the services of the professional. The general well-being of society would be very much harmed and economic activity would be very much inhibited if the quality of advice given depended significantly upon the particular members of the profession to whom an approach is made especially if that choice were to depend upon the posture of the professional—for example, pretending to be better able to give advice than other equally qualified persons or indicating a greater willingness to orientate that advice not to the needs of the problem but to the predilections of the client. It would be a very bad situation if the standard of medical care we received depended in any essential degree upon the chance choice of medical practitioners. There are bound to be some differences between one practitioner and another but it must be possible to assume that all practitioners have been educated to at least a common minimum level of diagnostic skill. It ought also to be possible to assume that skill is equally on offer from all qualified practitioners without fear or favour. If these assumptions cannot be made then instead of the uncertainty being taken out of our personal decisions as far as possible, the reverse would be the consequence. Life would be very much more hazardous.

All professional organizations that retain respect in the community exist to defend this respect by protecting the public interest. First by providing a system of professional training and examinations to qualify the actions of their members, i.e., to underwrite a minimum level of competence common to all those to whom they issue the qualification. Second by laying down a code of conduct that ensures impartiality and makes partiality a recognizable offence in respect of which a professional may be punished by his peers to the point of withdrawal of qualification. This is what professional education, therefore, is all about —competence and integrity.

Professional integrity is always difficult to define except in terms of specific situations in which honesty can be seen to be at risk and it is not amenable to classroom and examination room treatment. (For this reason the Institute of Actuaries which controls my own profession have thought it necessary to draft their code of conduct partly in general terms, but mainly in terms of recognizable and (from experience) likely situations which an actuary ought to avoid or about which the actuary should seek advice from the governing body of the profession before proceeding further.) It will be sufficient for the present to consider competence and the educational process which enables this to be underwritten.

Any system of professional training develops, each in its unique way, pre-existing ability and the major difficulty of designing a professional educational system is that of defining and increasing this ability. A superficial examination of most professional educational systems will give the impression, as one medical educationist recently put it, of simply drenching the student with information. But there is a great deal more to it than that. There has to be "drenching" so that past experience can be carried forward and so that appropriate techniques can be mastered. There is an old saying that "it is no good just being a genius, you have to be a genius at something". So there has to be a certain subject coverage and this coverage has to be continually adapted to contemporary practice (a problem in itself since practice in most professions is forever widening). The main objective however, is to select certain essential and innate qualities and to use the appropriate intellectual disciplines to develop them.

Perhaps I may briefly turn to my own profession, that of an Actuary, as an example. Kenneth Usherwood in his presidential address to the Institute of Actuaries of 1962 spoke of the need for an Actuary to have (in addition to personal integrity) "a capacity for clear and precise thinking and the prospect of developing a balanced judgement". This is perhaps the neatest description that has been made. The Actuary does need to have a superlative capacity for analysing a problem, usually in the field of financial planning, and for separating out the really important factors at work.

This capacity for analysing a situation and separating the important factors is a vital mental quality of the actuary; it can be developed and sharpened, but it must be there. It should be stressed that it is not merely a question of separating all the factors in a problem; it is a question as to their relative importance. The "balanced judgement" is a very important ingredient.

How do we select these qualities? As an indicator of clear thinking as well as a foundation for the subsequent building of a situation of essential techniques we call for a minimum mathematical ability. Next there is the first substantial stage of our examinations, the so-called intermediate stage which is designed partly to present a further process of selection and partly to commence the process of development of selected qualities. It may be claiming too much to regard these examinations as being so specifically designed. The examinations have evolved over the years (over 125 years) and have been shaped by successive review committees without necessarily such a simple or such an over-simplified view of their purpose. The subject coverage is important. We need to know a great deal about mathematics, statistics and economics and we bring the three subjects together as no other profession does. We do habitually use particular tools or techniques and we must be taught how to use them. It would be too much to claim that the subjects chosen are entirely so chosen with more than the objective of conveying familiarity with techniques but whether by design or by some process of natural selection these intermediate examinations do make heavy demands on clarity of thought. Those who cannot think clearly tend to find the going too hard. The examinations have evolved as an effective process of selection for actuarial potential.

The subjects included in the syllabus for the intermediate examinations look like problem solving, technique manipulating, subjects and some of the problems look a little esoteric but the problems are less important in themselves than as a medium for developing particular ways of thinking. It is fair to say therefore that what is taking place is more truly education than training. Because of their academic nature these subjects can be taught in the University and indeed my own installation as a Professor of Actuarial Science in the City University marks the beginning of the transfer of teaching from the profession itself to the university. We were rather slow to see the wisdom of this development and even slower to get the necessary financial resources.

For many years now almost all entrants to the profession have been university graduates so that the pre-intermediate process of selection has taken place at university; candidates have not attempted to enter the profession unless adequately equipped mathematically. The new development at the City University of an honours degree in actuarial science which exempts from the whole of the intermediate examinations brings the whole selection process forward in time to the university period. The exemption is subject to adequate performance in individual subject papers, which for the record cover numerical analysis, probability and statistics, compound interest, life contingencies, mortality and other actuarial investigations, and economics as a background to investment.

Beyond the intermediate stage there lies the final examinations which are not concerned with problem solving but are concerned with practice and judgement. There are a small number of entrants to the profession who having passed the intermediate examinations fail to pass or even do not attempt to pass the final examinations (which, broadly, cover life office, pension fund and investment practice) but very little further selection takes place at this stage. It is here that "balanced judgement" is being tested. There is a core of knowledge embodied in the official textbooks but the training is essentially practical and at the work bench.

We may now return to an important element of development—professional behaviour and the code of conduct. The tuition and examination system does not and cannot encompass this. Actuaries are concerned with financial planning in a highly competitive world in which the avoidance of self-interest and the maintenance of an independent professional view places strains upon integrity. If these strains are not met and held there can be immense public damage. As in all professions, individual actuaries guide, by the standards of behaviour they themselves maintain, the generations who follow them. Every actuary, is in this process, a teacher. Codes of behaviour are taught not in the classroom but in the working environment.

What has been said about the actuarial profession applies to all other professions that have any claim to call themselves professions. It is true for lawyers, doctors, dentists, nurses, architects, engineers and an expanding range of other professions. The techniques and skills differ and there are differences of emphasis in some of the qualities required. The system of education is not only a drenching with information but a process of selecting for innate qualities.

What do we expect of the manager? Two of the most important qualities are: First, an understanding of the overall objectives of the organisation; second, the ability to use information. The first is not only essential if there is to be anything to manage, it is also the focus of information provision and utilization. Before information can be used to generate alternative courses of action and to predict the likely consequences, it has to be provided. Before the professional can use his skills to assist the policy-making process, the manager must be articulate about his objectives and his strategic problems. He must be prepared to express his problems in terms which the professional understands: He must when necessary be prepared to translate the language associated with his management situation into terms which the professional can in turn convert to information requirements.

The manager must be prepared, assuming that the professional has done his job properly, to examine the action implications of the facts presented to him. The manager must be prepared to abandon the experience theory of management which, it has been said, was invented to keep the bad manager in existence. He must be prepared to learn quickly and to adapt quickly. This calls for a high degree of intelligence and courage.

There are certain qualities of personality that have to be selected for in the process of educating the manager. The manager innovates by the natural exercise of his group leadership, so that leadership is an important quality. The good manager must be prepared to trust his professional advisers provided that he can be sure that they are technically competent and truly professional in their approach just as he also entrusts his managerial subordinates with authority. The manager who cannot delegate cannot be advised and cannot decide.

It follows from all this that the education of the manager has to develop certain abilities in persons who are of high intelligence and have characteristics of leadership and decisiveness. The ability to use information is a natural extension of intelligence as is also the capacity to be able to recognize and define management problems. The manager in order to understand the objectives of the organization must have his own "drenching with information" sometimes of a highly technical nature. It is questionable whether he needs any education beyond this. A great deal of money is currently spent in putting managers through training courses in so called management techniques; for example, "management by objectives". These expositions are rather boring, laboured over-formalizations of what a manager must be able to do intuitively without a check-list to help him. There is something in management and someone had to try to define it in order that the education of the manager could become a rational process. That much was important. Unfortunately, putting a set of instructions on the packet is now a vested educational interest. It has become profitable to extend the instructions to a set of formal structures with fancy names, new names being inverted when the old ones have lost their novelty. Management training has suffered by being oversold.

The good manager does not need to pretend to be a professional. Many professionals make good managers when they decide to change their roles. It is not however essential for a manager to have a prior training in one of the professions. He needs to be able to think in quantitative terms but he does not need to be trained as a statistician or an accountant. He needs to be able to understand the machinery of law but not to be trained as a lawyer. He needs to know how an engineer thinks and especially to be able himself to think in terms of systems but not be trained as a an engineer. In short there needs to be formed an intermediate position for the manager between being professional (which he is not) and being a gifted amateur (which is rarely sufficient).

# Unsolved Problems in Medical Education

## E. WILKES

*Department of Community Medicine,
University of Sheffield, Sheffield, England*

Medicine has always been a staunchly conservative profession, and although it can on occasion change its ways overnight, more commonly it moves slowly away from the old routine. Spiritually we put boiling pitch on open wounds, we cup and blister and we apply with nostalgia the searching clyster and the hungry leech. Leeches, incidentally, were still available in the casualty departments in my student days and my wife as a nurse was instructed in their use. Who knows what imposing and fashionable procedures now in vogue will be compulsorily retired after a lifespan infinitely shorter than that of the leech?

We are getting gradually accustomed to the rapid changes in medical technology and to the fact that most of the drugs we use now were quite unknown a quarter of a century ago—and may indeed have returned to a discreet obscurity after another decade. Many of the new improvements are of detail, and frequently demonstrate the law of diminishing returns by producing a 5% improvement at a 50% increase in cost. The pattern of human behaviour is also variable, so that despite the factual explosion the real changes seem often more social than scientific.

Thirty or forty years ago the medical student came, of course, from a good family. He was, despite that, something of a wild tearabout—not with the revolutionary fervour of the social scientist but with the more kittenish and innocent energies of the sixth-former. He worshipped rugby football and beer with Bacchanalian fervour, but eventually blundering through his finals, went at once to practice on a forelock-touching and compliant public, who only rarely took him to court.

133

If a hospital career was chosen, after qualification he would work for a few years at a Victorian intensity compounded of long hours and poor pay and fascinating rich clinical material. This was accepted happily enough for the experience and the responsibilities crammed into a very few years were a superb investment carrying, after perhaps a lean period, an assured status and a good income for the rest of his working life. Suddenly the harum-scarum student was the trusted pillar of society, bishop's confidant and churchwarden, cricketer and gentleman, making an enjoyably slow pilgrimage to a memorial service packed with patients, cliches and half-sincere eulogy.

We behave as if this still was the world: but the patients are keener on litigation and have a depressing tendency to be more up-to-date than their doctors who, in turn, are not necessarily a world away from fornication, atheism, clock-watching and even political demonstrations. One problem in medical education is to get the young student to honour the trust—the doctor is still uniquely trusted—whilst getting him to realize at the same time that he no longer has automatic status but has to go out and earn it, and that for all his equipment may be sterile and disposable, he and his ideals are not.

Doctors have always varied in quality, but perhaps never so much as today. The early skills may become redundant after a disappointingly short time. The clinical expertise that used gradually to be augmented until retirement is subject now to ceaseless change and re-learning. The pace is so vicious that outside their field most specialists after a few years are either inexperienced or out-of-date, and the general practitioner is both. The general practitioner is the referee, filtering off selected patients to modern therapy and protecting his patients from the dangerous enthusiasms of the specialist who may have taught him.

We ask the nearly impossible. The better the medical facilities, the more they will be used, so we perpetually make a rod for our own backs. General practitioners may need to see personally over a hundred patients in a day. We have therefore to educate our doctors to be teacher and counsellor, diagnostician and therapist, businessman and civil servant, careful employer and devoted lifelong student. We add to these somewhat unrealistic demands out-dated hospitals, total dependence on overseas doctors, a ludicrous neglect of general practice, deplorably poor inter-professional cooperation, inferior pay and conditions of service leading to the emigration of hundreds of high-quality colleagues. We add, again and lightheartedly, demands for extra services like family planning and abortion (vital perhaps but no extra resources are allotted for them), we take for granted minor chores from the signing of passport photographs to vaccination, and we demand sick notes for the 324 million working days certified as lost through sickness each year.

These problems demand the right people to live with them, and like any publican at an art exhibition we know exactly what we like. The right students for medicine, we say, must come from a wide and cultured background—we ignore their abysmally poor ability to communicate accurately or to write gracefully, and we tend to reject those who have not specialized early in subjects relevant to the pre-clinical studies, yet we still dare hanker for the educated student. They must be capable of an empathy sensitive enough to enter the twilight world of the mentally ill. They must have an independence and a conscientiousness that will make them leave a congenial dinner party to comfort a dying patient five miles up the valley, when no one is interested in whether they go or not, and the only audience will be themselves and their God. At the same time we need a toughness that permits us to walk unscathed through a day littered with broken bodies and broken hopes to a tea hearty enough to win Dr Johnson's approbation. And with all this there must be an intellectual capacity for clinical decision-making that can exploit without effort the gifts brought by science and technology to the art of medicine.

To choose these right candidates—and there may be 3,000 of them competing for 120 places—we use the embarrassingly humdrum tools of A-level grades and the headmaster's report. We accept that this is not quite good enough, we agree that we select badly, but none of us knows how to make the selection better with the time and resources available. The A-level results may not be objective but theirs is an injustice that is seen to be unjust, so there is a heart-warming random-ness about them that is politically acceptable, at any rate to the selectors, for they are becoming as hunted as any vice-chancellor. The lyricism of the headmaster's report clearly varies more with the headmaster than with the candidate. But together these allow us to reduce the number of applicants to manageable proportions, although in the process we will reject students who are welcomed into less popular faculties, and we reject, of course, without giving them an interview.

Medical schools change their systems of selection in detail but at any rate in the recent past some medical schools did not even interview their successful candidates. So convinced were they of the unscientific nature of this social interaction, the possible prejudices and the vari-ability of responses, that candidates were chosen sight unseen. This perhaps overstates the case for justice being blind. Mostly the selectors have submitted their spouses to a prolonged interview before selection, and even if the outcome was unsatisfactory the attempt was thought to be worth making. We accept that the interview cannot spot genius but it can detect the squinting red-nosed dwarf, further distinguished by the exuberance of his acne, who may be brilliantly clever but who is too shy to attempt serious cardiac resuscitation with several hundred spectators watching him fail. We still may accept him, but we know a little more about what we are getting: and on the whole the mute inglorious Miltons are not usually right in medicine. With us—and we are not alone here—the glib rather than the meek tend to inherit.

The selection of medical students is important for the public good but we must not be over-ambitious. Many of the saints would nowadays, with bumbling committee caution, not be allowed near a theological college. Julius Caesar would have had problems about driving his chariot since he was an epileptic; Pasteur and Darwin were poor students; Jung and Einstein were probably worse. The list of unpromising children and youths would include Reynolds, Gauguin, Manet, Rodin, Swift, Wordsworth, Keats, Yeats, Goldsmith, Tolstoy, and with fine impartiality both Napoleon and the Duke of Wellington and Winston Churchill (Illingworth, 1974).

We select students with the intimidating knowledge that this long and expensive course tends to get easier as it goes along. It is our wish to reject our obvious errors of selection early in the course or not at all. This means that the most difficult thing about a medical education is to be accepted by a medical school.

From whom are this elite chosen?

The Todd report (1968) found that in 1956 17% of medical students had medical fathers. Ten years later this had increased to over 21%. Clearly the doctors doing the selecting find this satisfactory. Less happily, such students may do badly in their examinations (Last and Stanley, 1969), since 18·5% of students with no medical family history had to repeat part of their examinations while 23·1% of students with a medical parent had to do so. Parental pressures towards doing medicine may be associated with this, especially as doctors' children seem to choose a medical career at an earlier age: but this is probably no more than a natural preference for the devil one knows.

With this bias towards doctors' children is naturally associated a preference, varying greatly in degree with different medical schools, for the public school product and the social class 1 background. Three per cent of social class 4 and 5 get accepted for medical school and I am aware of no evidence to suggest that they are more likely to burn it down. They are certainly more likely to pass their examinations, for three quarters of them in one survey passed all their tests at the first try and only half of the public schoolboys succeeded in doing this (Simpson, 1972). But examination successes are valueless as predictors of future professional distinction. There is more to life than examination results. In our examination system we tend to extract success from the neurotic introvert (Furneaux, 1961) and to penalize the stable extrovert who would be preferred by many as their doctor.

Lavin (1967) has suggested the personality variables that should be sought because of their association with success. These include high morale, social responsibility, stability, motivation, endurance, originality and class participation, with a low need for conformity to peer-group pressures. These factors we do not assess before or during training except as can be done in the everyday teacher-student contacts. These contacts will become even more diluted and unreliable with the increasing tendency to teach more and more medical students with fewer and fewer staff. An intake of 150 students is reputed to be the smallest economically viable number today (Sinclair, 1972) and Sinclair and many others feel that there is a continuous pressure on the medical schools to go for quantity rather than quality.

When we turn to the content of the medical curriculum, we see further areas of uncertainty and debate. Almost every medical school in the country comes into one of three categories: either they have refused to change their curriculum, or they are thinking soon of changing their curriculum, or they are licking their wounds after recently doing so. The traditional sequence in medical education is to spend the first preclinical years in the study of basic medical sciences—anatomy, physiology, biochemistry, pathology, and so on. After the preclinical examination is passed, much of this basic knowledge is jettisoned by the student with the speed of a marathon runner throwing away a drinking cup: and they turn with relief to real patients with real problems.

This is a tragic waste and the more modern curricula reject this concept of a customs-barrier between preclinical and clinical work. Even the traditional curricula seek to modify the separation with case-demonstrations and episodes of multidisciplinary topic-teaching, rationed by the expensiveness of such exercises in teacher-hours; but few schools have solved the problem of keeping the basic sciences exciting and relevant to the students' clinical learning. The teaching of some of these subjects by academics who are not fully in touch with the interests of tomorrow's doctors—biochemists, psychologists and sociologists are most criticized for this—obviously adds to the problem, and replaces old merely with new tyrants, equally rejected and resented by the students.

The process of change in the timetable is also as slow as it is bitter. Simpson (1972) puts it succinctly when he says that "until recently anatomy departments exacted a sort of *droit de seigneur* of 900 hours". The yardstick of student-hours, the fight for status and the factual explosion all lead to learned professors in faculty discussing the allocation of time with the tolerant consideration of hyenas quarrelling over a dead horse.

Students tend to sacrifice their interests to the passing at all costs of examinations, and this cannot be generally helpful to their higher education. It does mean that their knowledge is closely guided by the interests of their teachers, since these may well be over-represented in the examinations. This tends to perpetuate the present system of medical care based mainly on the attitudes and enthusiasms of the doctors while ignoring dangerously the real needs of society. Despite this, tremendous effort is put into timetabling the syllabus, and "covering the syllabus", if one can quote Simpson (1972) again, "has become a task as onerous and accompanied by even more sweating and heavy breathing as covering a mare—but much less fruitful".

The teaching qualities of the medical staff are almost totally ignored in their recruitment. Despite the importance of enthusiasm, clarity and good student relationships, only the research potential of the lecturer is carefully assessed. This means that modern teaching techniques—the lively seminar, programmed learning, the organization of small-group teaching or student projects, videotapes and tape-slide libraries—are not properly exploited even now in many schools. The service commitments of the more expensive and fascinating departments—ultrasonics in obstetrics, radioisotopes in cancer diagnosis, immunochemistry in the prenatal diagnosis of foetal abnormality, computers in survey work, X-ray scanners in neurology—may force the school to fob off the large class with a smoked drum and a frog's leg preparation redolent of the interests of half a century ago.

If we are not sure who to teach, how to teach or what to teach, can we assess what the medical student has actually learned? Half the graduates in one group questioned (Lyden *et al.*, 1968) criticized their training as failing to meet their needs, and predictably the general practitioners were more critical than those in specialist practice. Certainly some examinations seem most effective in testing the students' capacity for isolated factual recall, and failure rates vary from $1 \cdot 1\%$ at Newcastle to $10 \cdot 5\%$ at Liverpool.

Not many schools can better the Birmingham system of continuous assessment. Frequent tests in the preclinical course include short essays, true-false and multiple choice questions, practical and project work, while in the clinical course different methods test clinical skills, history-taking and attitudes. Longer elective periods are helpful in encouraging the students' individual development and are especially valuable for students near the end of their course. These elective periods allow them to see something of the tremendous variety in medicine. Different qualities are demanded of the regimental officer or the ship's doctor as compared to the pathologist, the administrator, or the psychiatrist. This variety also makes difficult a good understanding between widely differing medical departments, and the basic principles of one professor may seem trivia to another. That I feel that key problems tend to be ignored, that an inadequate amount of attention is directed to the determination of priorities in medical care, to the description of different health care systems, to the sociology of prescribing and the doctor-patient relationship, to the art of counselling, to the contributions of other professions—all these may be mere minutiae to some of my colleagues.

This allows many doctors to ignore the fact that modern medicine creates more problems than it solves. The prolongation of handicapped life, the creation of new facilities such as the replacement arthroplasty of hip or renal dialysis without the back-up that will make these properly available is a problem that takes some doctors by surprise. A measles immunization campaign mounted in a highly susceptible primitive community without, at the same time, improved agricultural technology and a family planning service would replace the traditionally acceptable death of children through measles with the politically more explosive and physically more protracted death by starvation. One could go through some schools without realizing that in a complex and overcrowded world there is more to medicine nowadays than putting up one's plate.

And yet having said all this, good doctors come from our medical schools. This may be because to some extent they have selected and educated themselves: but it is likely also that no matter how their curriculum is made up, they have learnt much from watching dedicated and intelligent doctors at work, and also by contact with patients so often characterized by a racy informativeness, a dignity and a courage worth a mountain of scissors-and-paste textbooks to our callow and inexperienced young scientists.

Even in today's world, the doctors do not lightly ape the sleazier behaviour-patterns of our society. They temper their greed with mercy and they carry their burdens with responsibility and humour. We have failed to teach them attitudes of lifelong learning, but even here we can quote Sir Thomas Browne in palliation:

"Knowledge is made by oblivion, and to purchase a clear and warrantable body of Truth, we must forget and part with much we know."

So it could be that one of the most difficult problems in medical education is not what to learn at all, but what, in a changing world, to forget.

## References

Furneaux, W. D. (1961). *The Chosen Few: An Examination of Some Aspects of University Selection in Britain*. London: Oxford University Press.
Illingworth, R. (1974). *Practitioner*, **213,** 303.
Last, J. M. and Stanley, G. R. (1969). *British Journal Medical Education*, **3,** 43.
Lavin, D. E. (1967). *The Prediction of Academic Performance*. New York: Wiley.
Lyden, F. J., Geiger, H. J. and Paterson, O. L. (1968). *The Training of Good Physicians*. Cambridge, Mass: Harvard University Press.
Simpson, M. A. (1972). *Medical Education: A Critical Approach*. London: Butterworth.
Sinclair, D. A. (1972). *Basic Medical Education*. London: Oxford University Press.
Todd, Lord (Chairman) (1968). *Report of the Royal Commission on Medical Education*. London: HMSO Cmnd. 3569.

# Index